Recife
Northeast
Brazil

Alex Robinson

Credits

Footprint credits

Editor: Alan Murphy
Production and layout: Patrick Dawson, Elysia Alim, Danielle Bricker
Maps: Kevin Feeney

Managing Director: Andy Riddle
Commercial Director: Patrick Dawson
Publisher: Alan Murphy
Publishing Managers: Felicity Laughton, Nicola Gibbs
Digital Editors: Jo Williams, Tom Mellors
Marketing and PR: Liz Harper
Sales: Diane McEntee
Advertising: Renu Sibal
Finance and Administration: Elizabeth Taylor

Photography credits

Front cover: Giancarlo Liguori/Shutterstock
Back cover: Gustavo Fadel/Shutterstock

Printed in Great Britain by CPI Antony Rowe, Chippenham, Wiltshire

Every effort has been made to ensure that the facts in this guidebook are accurate. However, travellers should still obtain advice from consulates, airlines etc about travel and visa requirements before travelling. The authors and publishers cannot accept responsibility for any loss, injury or inconvenience however caused.

Publishing information

Footprint *Focus Recife & Northeast Brazil*
1st edition
© Footprint Handbooks Ltd
July 2011

ISBN: 978 1 908206 03 9
CIP DATA: A catalogue record for this book is available from the British Library

® Footprint Handbooks and the Footprint mark are a registered trademark of Footprint Handbooks Ltd

Published by Footprint
6 Riverside Court
Lower Bristol Road
Bath BA2 3DZ, UK
T +44 (0)1225 469141
F +44 (0)1225 469461
footprinttravelguides.com

Distributed in the USA by Globe Pequot Press, Guilford, Connecticut

The content of Footprint *Focus Recife & Northeast Brazil* has been taken directly from Footprint's *Brazil Handbook*, which was written and researched by Alex Robinson.

Contents

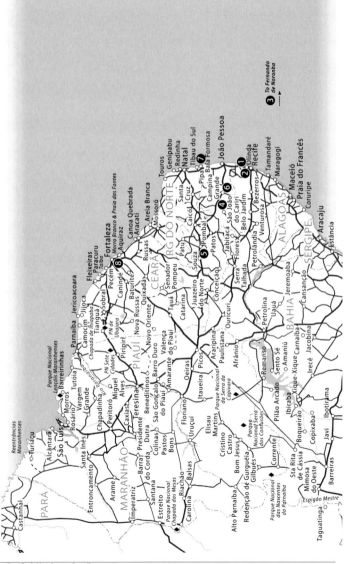

The northeast of Brazil is often overlooked by visitors. But those who spend time in the region, exploring its buildings, sampling the music and arts scene in Recife or getting lost in the crowds at the great festivals in the *sertão* find it one of the most interesting, diverse and least spoilt parts of Brazil.

In the first centuries of its colonial history, the region grew rich through sugar and became the commercial and intellectual centre of Brazil. Pernambuco, in particular, retains many magnificent buildings from that period, while the convents in Olinda and Igarassu are fine examples of Iberian baroque. The region has never been more culturally exciting than today. In the 1990s Recife saw the explosion of an artistic movement called *mangue beat*, which sought to fuse the rich heritage of Pernambuco folk art and music with social activism and post-modernism. The resulting cultural fluorescence has helped to make Pernambuco Brazil's most vibrant cultural state. Carnaval in Recife or Olinda is considered by many to be the best and most traditional in the country.

Bahia may have the prettiest stretches of coastline in Brazil but the northeast has some of the most dramatic. In Rio Grande do Norte, broken, striated cliffs and imposing dunes tower above the wild and deserted beaches of Natal, Genipabu, Pipa and Areia Branca. In neighbouring Ceará the coast becomes touristy again, especially around the state capital, Fortaleza, a sunny, planned city whose charm is somewhat sullied by a plethora of cheap package tours.

Planning your trip

Getting there

Air
Flights into Brazil generally land in São Paulo or Rio de Janeiro but Fortaleza and Recife have connections to the USA and Europe. Prices are cheapest in October, November and after Carnaval and at their highest in the European summer and the Brazilian high seasons (generally 15 December to 15 January, the Thursday before Carnaval to the Saturday after Carnaval, and 15 June to 15 August).

Air passes
TAM and GOL offer a 21-day **Brazil Airpass**, which is valid on any TAM destination within Brazil. The price varies according to the number of flights taken and the international airline used to arrive in Brazil. They can only be bought outside Brazil. One to four flights start at around US$540, five flights start at US$680, six flights start at US$840, seven flights start at US$990, eight flights start at US$1120, and nine flights start at US$1259. The baggage allowance is the same as that permitted on their international flights. TAM and Gol also operate as part of the **Mercosur Airpass**, which is valid for Brazil, Argentina, Chile, Uruguay and Paraguay using local carriers. It is valid for any passenger with a return ticket to their country of origin, and must be bought with an international flight. The minimum stay is seven days, maximum 45 and at least two countries must be visited. The maximum number of flights is eight. Fares, worked out on a mileage basis, cost between US$295 and US$1195. Children pay a discounted rate, and under-threes pay 10% of the adult rate. Some of the carriers operate a blackout period between 15 December and 15 January.

Baggage allowance
Airlines will only allow a certain weight of luggage without a surcharge; for Brazil this is usually two items of 32 kg but may be as low as 20 kg; with two items of hand luggage weighing up to 10 kg in total. UK airport staff can refuse to load bags weighing more than 30 kg. Baggage allowances are higher in business and first class. Weight limits for internal flights are often lower, usually 20 kg. In all cases it is best to enquire beforehand.

Getting around

Public transport in Brazil is very efficient, but distances are huge. Most visitors will find themselves travelling by buses and planes, except in the Amazon when a boat is often the only way to get around. Train routes are practically non-existent, car hire is expensive and hitchhiking not advisable. Taxis vary widely in quality and price but are easy to come by and safe when taken from a *posto de taxis* (taxi rank).

Air
Because of the size of the country, flying is often the most practical option and internal air services are highly developed. All state capitals and larger cities are linked with each other with services several times a day, and all national airlines offer excellent service. Recent

Don't miss ...

deregulation of the airlines has greatly reduced prices on some routes and low-cost airlines offer fares that can often be as cheap as travelling by bus (when booked through the internet). Paying with an international credit card is not always possible online; but it is usually possible to buy an online ticket through a hotel, agency or willing friend without surcharge. Many of the smaller airlines go in and out of business sporadically. GOL, Oceanair, TAM, TRIP/Total, Varig, and Webjet operate the most extensive routes. Most of their websites (see below) provide full information, including a booking service, although not all are in English.

Rail

There are 30,379 km of railways, which are not combined into a unified system; almost all run goods trains only. Brazil has two gauges and there is little transfer between them. Two more gauges exist for the isolated **Amapá** railway (used to transport manganese from the Serra do Navio) and the tourist-only **São João del Rei** and **Ouro Preto-Mariana** lines. There is also the **Trem do Pantanal** – a tourist-designated train running between Campo Grande and Miranda in the Pantanal.

Road

The best paved highways are heavily concentrated in the southeast, but roads serving the interior are being improved to all-weather status and many are paved. Most main roads between principal cities are paved. Some are narrow and therefore dangerous; many are in poor condition.

Bus

There are three standards of bus: *Comum*, or *Convencional*, are quite slow, not very comfortable and fill up quickly; *Executivo* are more expensive, comfortable (many have reclining seats), and don't stop en route to pick up passengers so are safer; *Leito* (literally 'bed') run at night between the main centres, offering reclining seats with leg rests, toilets, and sometimes refreshments, at double the normal fare. For journeys over 100 km, most buses have chemical toilets (bring toilet paper). Air conditioning can make buses cold at night, so take a jumper; on some services blankets are supplied.

Buses stop fairly frequently (every two to four hours) at *postos* for snacks. Bus stations for interstate services and other long-distance routes are called *rodoviárias*. They are frequently outside the city centres and offer snack bars, lavatories, left luggage, local bus services and information centres. Buy bus tickets at *rodoviárias* (most now take credit cards), not from travel agents who add on surcharges. Reliable bus information is hard to come by, other than from companies themselves. Buses usually arrive and depart in very good time. Many town buses have turnstiles, which can be inconvenient if you are carrying a large pack. Urban buses normally serve local airports.

Car

Car hire Renting a car in Brazil is expensive: the cheapest rate for unlimited mileage for a small car is about US$65 per day. These costs can be more than halved by reserving a car over the internet through one of the larger international companies such as Europcar (www.europcar.co.uk) or Avis (www.avis.co.uk). Minimum age for renting a car is 21 and it's essential to have a credit card. Companies operate under the terms *aluguel de automóveis* or *auto-locadores*. Check exactly what the company's insurance policy covers. In many cases it will not cover major accidents or 'natural' damage (eg flooding). Ask if extra cover is available. Sometimes using a credit card automatically includes insurance. Beware of being billed for scratches that were on the vehicle before you hired it.

Taxi

Rates vary from city to city, but are consistent within each city. At the outset, make sure the meter is cleared and shows 'tariff 1', except (usually) from 2300-0600, Sunday, and in December when '2' is permitted. Check that the meter is working; if not, fix the price in advance. The **radio taxi** service costs about 50% more but cheating is less likely. Taxis outside larger hotels usually cost more. If you are seriously cheated, note the number of the taxi and insist on a signed bill; threatening to take it to the police can work. **Mototaxis** are much more economical, but many are unlicensed and there have been a number of robberies of passengers.

Sleeping

There is a good range of accommodation options in Brazil. An *albergue* or hostel offers the cheapest option. These have dormitory beds and single and double rooms. Many are part of the IYHA, www.iyha.org. **Hostel world**, www.hostelworld.com; **Hostel Bookers**, www.hostelbookers.com; and **Hostel.com**, www.hostel.com, are useful portals. **Hostel Trail Latin America** – T0131-208 0007 (UK), www.hosteltrail.com – managed from their hostel in Popayan, is an online network of hotels and tour companies in South America. A *pensão* is either a cheap guesthouse or a household that rents out some rooms.

A *pousada* is either a bed-and-breakfast, often small and family-run, or a sophisticated and often charming small hotel. A *hotel* is as it is anywhere else in the world, operating according to the international star system, although five-star hotels are not price controlled and hotels in any category are not always of the standard of their star equivalent in the USA, Canada or Europe. Many of the older hotels can be cheaper than hostels. Usually accommodation prices include a breakfast of rolls, ham, cheese, cakes and fruit with coffee and juice; there is no reduction if you don't eat it. Rooms vary too. Normally an *apartamento* is a room with separate living and sleeping areas and sometimes cooking facilities. A *quarto* is a standard room; *com banheiro* is en suite; and

Sleeping and eating price codes

Sleeping

$$$$ over US$150		**$$$**	US$66-150
$$ US$30-65		**$**	Under US$30

Prices include taxes and service charge, but not meals. They are based on a double room, except in the **$** range, where prices are almost always per person.

Eating

†††	Expensive over US$20	††	Mid-range US$8-20
†	Cheap under US$8		

Prices refer to the cost of a two-course meal, not including drinks.

sem banheiro is with shared bathroom. Finally there are the *motels*. These should not be confused with their US counterpart: motels are used by guests not intending to sleep; there is no stigma attached and they usually offer good value (the rate for a full night is called the '*pernoite*'), however the decor can be a little garish.

It's a good idea to book accommodation in advance in small towns that are popular at weekends with city dwellers (eg near São Paulo and Rio de Janeiro), and it's essential to book at peak times.

Luxury accommodation

Much of the luxury private accommodation sector can be booked through operators. **Angatu**, www.angatu.com, offers the best private homes along the Costa Verde, together with bespoke trips. **Dehouche**, www.dehouche.com, offers upmarket accommodation and trips in Bahia, Rio and Alagoas. **Brazilian Beach House**, www.brazilianbeachhouse.com, has some of the finest houses in Búzios and Trancoso but is not so great at organizing transfers and pick-ups. **Matuete**, www.matuete.com, has a range of luxurious properties and tours throughout Brazil.

Camping

Those with an international camping card pay only half the rate of a non-member at **Camping Clube do Brasil** sites, www.campingclube.com.br. Membership of the club itself is expensive: US$85 for six months. The club has 43 sites in 13 states and 80,000 members. It may be difficult to get into some Camping Clube campsites during high season (January to February). Private campsites charge about US$8-15 per person. For those on a very low budget and in isolated areas where there is no campsite available, it's usually possible to stay at service stations. They have shower facilities, watchmen and food; some have dormitories. There are also various municipal sites. Campsites tend to be some distance from public transport routes and are better suited to people with their own car. Wild camping is generally difficult and dangerous. Never camp at the side of a road; this is very risky.

Homestays

Staying with a local family is an excellent way to become integrated quickly into a city and companies try to match guests to their hosts. **Cama e Café**, www.camaecafe.com.br, organizes homestays in Rio de Janeiro, Olinda and a number of other cities around Brazil. **Couch surfing**, www.couchsurfing.com, offers a free, backpacker alternative.

Quality hotel associations
The better international hotel associations have members in Brazil. These include: **Small Luxury Hotels of the World**, www.slh.com; the **Leading Hotels of the World**, www.lhw.com; the **Leading Small Hotels of the World**, www.leadingsmallhotels oftheworld.com; **Great Small Hotels**, www.greatsmallhotels.com; and the **French Relais et Chateaux group**, www.relaischateaux.com, which also includes restaurants.

The Brazilian equivalent of these associations is the **Roteiros de Charme**, www.roteiros decharme.com.br, with some 30 locations in the southeast and northeast. Whilst membership of these groups pretty much guarantees quality, it is by no means comprehensive. There are many fine hotels and charming *pousadas* listed in our text that are not included in these associations.

Online travel agencies (OTAs)
Services like **Tripadvisor** and OTAs associated with them – such as **hotels.com, expedia.com** and **venere.com**, are well worth using for both reviews and for booking ahead. Hotels booked through an OTA can be up to 50% cheaper than the rack rate. Similar sites operate for hostels (though discounts are far less considerable). They include the **Hostelling International** site, www.hihostels.com, **hostelbookers.com, hostels.com** and **hostelworld.com**.

Eating and drinking

Food
Brazilians consider their cuisine to be up there with the world's best. Visitors may disagree. Mains are generally heavy, meaty and unspiced. Deserts are often very sweet. That said, the best cooking south of the Rio Grande is in São Paulo and Rio, where a heady mix of international immigrants has resulted in some unusual fusion cooking and exquisite variations on French, Japanese, Portuguese, Arabic and Italian traditional techniques and dishes. The regional cooking in Pará is also a delight – utilizing unusual and unique fruits and vegetables from the Amazon and the sumptuous Amazonian river fish.

Outside the more sophisticated cities it can be a struggle to find interesting food. The Brazilian staple meal generally consists of a cut of fried or barbecued meat, chicken or fish accompanied by rice, black or South American broad beans and an unseasoned salad of lettuce, grated carrot, tomato and beetroot. Condiments are weak chilli sauce, olive oil, salt and pepper and vinegar.

The national dish is a greasy campfire stew called *feijoada*, made by throwing jerked beef, smoked sausage, tongue and salt pork into a pot with lots of fat and beans and stewing it for hours. The resulting stew is sprinkled with fried *farofa* (manioc flour) and served with *couve* (kale) and slices of orange. The meal is washed down with *cachaça* (sugarcane rum). Most restaurants serve the *feijoada completa* for Saturday lunch (up until about 1630). Come with a very empty stomach.

Brazil's other national dish is mixed grilled meat or *churrasco*, served in vast portions off the spit by legions of rushing waiters, and accompanied by a buffet of salads, beans and mashed vegetables. *Churrascos* are served in *churrascarias* or *rodízios*. The meat is generally excellent, especially in the best *churascarias*, and the portions are unlimited, offering good value for camel-stomached carnivores able to eat one meal a day.

In remembrance of Portugal, but bizarrely for a tropical country replete with fish, Brazil is also the world's largest consumer of **cod**, pulled from the cold north Atlantic, salted and served in watery slabs or little balls as *bacalhau* (an appetizer/bar snack) or *petisco*. Other national *petiscos* include *kibe* (a deep-fried or baked mince with onion, mint and flour), *coxinha* (deep-fried chicken or meat in dough), *empadas* (baked puff-pastry patties with prawns, chicken, heart of palm or meat), and *tortas* (little pies with the same ingredients). When served in bakeries, *padarias* or snack bars these are collectively referred to as *salgadinhos* (savouries).

Eating cheaply

The cheapest dish is the *prato feito* or *sortido*, an excellent-value set menu usually comprising meat/chicken/fish, beans, rice, chips and salad. The *prato comercial* is similar but rather better and a bit more expensive. Portions are usually large enough for two and come with two plates. If you are on your own, you could ask for an *embalagem* (doggy bag) or a *marmita* (takeaway) and offer it to a person with no food (many Brazilians do). Many restaurants serve *comida por kilo* buffets where you serve yourself and pay for the weight of food on your plate. This is generally good value and is a good option for vegetarians. *Lanchonetes* and *padarias* (diners and bakeries) are good for cheap eats; usually serving *prato feitos*, *salgadinhos*, excellent juices and other snacks.

The main meal is usually taken in the middle of the day; cheap restaurants tend not to be open in the evening.

Drink

The national liquor is *cachaça* (also known as *pinga*), which is made from sugar-cane, and ranging from cheap supermarket and service-station fire-water, to boutique distillery and connoisseur labels from the interior of Minas Gerais. Mixed with fruit juice, sugar and crushed ice, *cachaça* becomes the principal element in a *batida*, a refreshing but deceptively powerful drink. Served with pulped lime or other fruit, mountains of sugar and smashed ice it becomes the world's favourite party cocktail, caipirinha. A less potent caipirinha made with vodka is called a *caipiroska* and with sake a *saikirinha* or *caipisake*.

Brazilian beer is generally lager, served ice-cold. Draught beer is called *chope* or *chopp* (after the German Schoppen, and pronounced 'shoppi'). There are various national brands of bottled beers, which include Brahma, Skol, Cerpa, Antartica and the best Itaipava and Bohemia. There are black beers too, notably Xingu. They tend to be sweet. The best beer is from the German breweries in Rio Grande do Sul and is available only there.

Brazil's myriad fruits are used to make fruit juices or *sucos*, which come in a delicious variety, unrivalled anywhere in the world. *Açai*, *acerola*, *caju* (cashew), *pitanga*, *goiaba* (guava), *genipapo*, *graviola* (*chirimoya*), *maracujá* (passion fruit), *sapoti*, *umbu* and *tamarindo* are a few of the best. *Vitaminas* are thick fruit or vegetable drinks with milk. *Caldo de cana* is sugar-cane juice, sometimes mixed with ice. *Água de côco* or *côco verde* is coconut water served straight from a chilled, fresh, green coconut. The best known of many local soft drinks is *guaraná*, which is a very popular carbonated fruit drink, completely unrelated to the Amazon nut. The best variety is *guaraná Antarctica*. Coffee is ubiquitous and good tea entirely absent.

How big is your footprint?

→ Where possible choose a destination, tour operator or hotel with a proven ethical and environmental commitment – if in doubt, ask.

→ Spend money on locally produced (rather than imported) goods and services, buy directly from the producer or from a 'fair trade' shop, and use common sense when bargaining – the few dollars you save may be a week's salary to others.

→ Use water and electricity carefully – travellers may receive preferential supply while the needs of local communities are overlooked.

→ Learn about local etiquette and culture – consider local norms and behaviour and dress appropriately for local cultures and situations.

→ Protect wildlife and other natural resources – don't buy souvenirs or goods unless they are sustainably produced and are not protected under CITES legislation.

→ Always ask before taking photographs or videos of people.

→ Consider staying in local accommoda- tion rather than foreign-owned hotels – the economic benefits for host commu- nities are greater – and there are more opportunities to learn about local culture.

→ Within cities, local buses and (in São Paulo) metrôs are fast, cheap and have extensive routes. Try one instead of a taxi, and meet some real Brazilians!

→ Long-distance buses may take longer than flying but they have comfortable reclining seats, some offer drinks, and show up-to-date DVDs. They may have better schedules too.

→ Supermarkets will give you a plastic bag for even the smallest purchases. If you don't need one, let them know – plastic waste is a huge problem – particularly in the northeast. When buying certain drinks, look for the returnable glass bottles.

→ Make a voluntary contribution to Climate Care, www.co2.org, to help counteract the pollution caused by tax-free fuel on your flight.

Responsible travel

Sustainable or ecotourism is not just about looking after the physical environment, but also the local community. Whilst it has been slow to catch up with Costa Rica or Ecuador, Brazil now has some first-rate ecotourism projects and the country is a pioneer in urban community tourism in the favelas. Model ecotourism resorts in the forest include **Pousada Uacari** and **Cristalino Jungle Lodge. Fazenda San Francisco** in the Pantanal runs a pioneering jaguar conservation project; **REGUA** and **Serra dos Tucanos** on the Atlantic coast have done a great deal to protect important birding habitats; and resorts such as **Mata N'ativa** in Trancoso are taking important first steps in beach holiday areas. In the Amazon, Atlantic coast forest and parts of the *cerrado*, access to certain wilderness areas is restricted to scientists. Having such a low-impact policy over these regions means that their environment is protected from damage or over-use. In much of coastal Brazil, where tourism and property speculation has boomed in the last few years, the impact on local communities is particularly devastating. Some state governments cheerfully exploit the colourful local culture while sharing little of the profit. So rather than staying in a big resort and organizing a tour from back home, seek out smaller locally owned hotels and local indigenous guides. Try to visit projects such as the **Pataxó Reserve** in Jaqueira, Porto Seguro, and support the Caiçaras near Paraty.

Essentials A-Z

Accident and emergency
Ambulance T192. **Police** T190. If robbed or attacked, contact the tourist police. If you need to claim on insurance, make sure you get a police report.

Electricity
Generally 110 V 60 cycles AC, but in some cities and areas 220 V 60 cycles AC is used. European and U.S 2-pin plugs and sockets.

Embassies and consulates
For embassies and consulates of Brazil, see www.embassiesabroad.com.

Health → *Hospitals/medical services are listed in the Directory sections.*
See your GP or travel clinic at least 6 weeks before departure for general advice on travel risks and vaccinations. Try phoning a specialist travel clinic if your own doctor is unfamiliar with health in the region. Make sure you have sufficient medical travel insurance, get a dental check, know your own blood group and, if you suffer a long-term condition such as diabetes or epilepsy, obtain a **Medic Alert** bracelet (www.medicalalert.co.uk).

Vaccinations and anti-malarials
Confirm that your primary courses and boosters are up to date. It is advisable to vaccinate against polio, tetanus, typhoid, hepatitis A and, for more remote areas, rabies. Yellow fever vaccination is obligatory for most areas. Cholera, diptheria and hepatitis B vaccinations are sometimes advised. Specialist advice should be taken on the best antimalarials to take before you leave.

Health risks
The major risks posed in the region are those caused by insect disease carriers such as mosquitoes and sandflies. The key parasitic and viral diseases are malaria, South American trypanosomiasis (Chagas disease) and dengue fever. Be aware that you are always at risk from these diseases. **Malaria** is a danger throughout the lowland tropics and coastal regions. **Dengue fever** (which is currently rife in Rio de Janeiro state) is particularly hard to protect against as the mosquitoes can bite throughout the day as well as night (unlike those that carry malaria); try to wear clothes that cover arms and legs and also use effective mosquito repellent. Mosquito nets dipped in permethrin provide a good physical and chemical barrier at night. **Chagas disease** is spread by faeces of the triatomine, or assassin bugs, whereas sandflies spread a disease of the skin called **leishmaniasis**.

Some form of **diarrhoea** or intestinal upset is almost inevitable, the standard advice is always to wash your hands before eating and to be careful with drinking water and ice; if you have any doubts about the water then boil it or filter and treat it. In a restaurant buy bottled water or ask where the water has come from. Food can also pose a problem, be wary of salads if you don't know whether they have been washed or not.

There is a constant threat of **tuberculosis** (TB) and although the BCG vaccine is available, it is still not guaranteed protection. It is best to avoid unpasteurized dairy products and try not to let people cough and splutter all over you.

Another risk, especially to campers and people with small children, is that of the **hanta virus**, which is carried by some forest and riverine rodents. Symptoms are a flu-like illness which can lead to complications. Try as far as possible to avoid rodent-infested areas, especially close contact with rodent droppings.

Money
Currency

→ *£1 = R$2.65; €1 = R$2.38; US$1 = R$1.6 (May 2011).* The unit of currency is the **real**, R$ (plural **reais**). Any amount of foreign currency and 'a reasonable sum' in reais can be taken in, but sums over US$10,000 must be declared. Residents may only take out the equivalent of US$4000. Notes in circulation are: 100, 50, 10, 5 and 1 real; coins: 1 real, 50, 25, 10, 5 and 1 centavo. **Note** The exchange-rate fluctuates – check regularly.

Costs of travelling

Brazil is more expensive than other countries in South America. As a very rough guide, prices are about two-thirds those of Western Europe and a little cheaper than rural USA; though prices vary hugely according to the current exchange rate and strength of the real, whose value has soared since 2008 – with Goldman Sachs and Bloomberg considering the *real* to be the most over-valued major currency in the world in 2009-2010. It is expected to lose value; check on the latest before leaving on currency exchange sites such as www.x-rates.com.

Hostel beds are usually around US$15. Budget hotels with few frills have rooms for as little as US$30, and you should have no difficulty finding a double room costing US$45 wherever you are. Rooms are often pretty much the same price whether 1 or 2 people are staying. Eating is generally inexpensive, especially in *padarias* or *comida por kilo* (pay by weight) restaurants, which offer a wide range of food (salads, meat, pasta, vegetarian). Expect to pay around US$6 to eat your fill in a good-value restaurant. Although bus travel is cheap by US or European standards, because of the long distances, costs can soon mount up. Internal flights prices have come down dramatically in the last couple of years and some routes work out cheaper than taking a bus – especially if booking through the internet. Prices vary regionally. Ipanema is almost twice as expensive as rural Bahia. A can of beer in a supermarket in the southeast costs US$0.80, a litre of water US$0.60, a single metrô ticket in São Paulo US$1.60, a bus ticket between US$1 and US$1.50 (depending on the city) and a cinema ticket around US$3.60.

ATMs

ATMs, or cash machines, are common in Brazil. As well as being the most convenient way of withdrawing money, they frequently offer the best available rates of exchange. They are usually closed after 2130 in large cities. There are 2 international ATM acceptance systems, **Plus** and **Cirrus**. Many issuers of debit and credit cards are linked to one, or both (eg Visa is Plus, MasterCard is Cirrus). **Bradesco** and **HSBC** are the 2 main banks offering this service. **Red Banco 24 Horas** kiosks advertise that they take a long list of credit cards in their ATMs, including MasterCard and Amex, but international cards cannot always be used; the same is true of **Banco do Brasil**.

Advise your bank before leaving, as cards are usually stopped in Brazil without prior warning. Find out before you leave what international functionality your card has. Check if your bank or credit card company imposes handling charges. Internet banking is useful for monitoring your account or transferring funds. Do not rely on 1 card, in case of loss. If you do lose a card, immediately contact the 24-hr helpline of the issuer in your home country (keep this number in a safe place).

Exchange

Banks in major cities will change cash and traveller's cheques (TCs). If you keep the official exchange slips, you may convert back into foreign currency up to 50% of the amount you exchanged. The parallel market, found in travel agencies, exchange houses and among hotel staff, often offers marginally better rates than the banks but commissions can be very high. Many banks may only change US$300 minimum in cash, US$500 in TCs. Rates for TCs are usually far lower than for cash, they are harder to change and a very heavy commission may be charged. Dollars cash (take US$5 or US$10 bills) are not useful as alternative currency. Brazilians use *reais*.

Credit cards

Credit cards are widely used, although often they are not usable in the most unlikely of places, such as tour operators. **Diners Club**, **MasterCard**, **Visa** and **Amex** are useful. Cash advances on credit cards will only be paid in *reais* at the tourist rate, incurring at least a 1.5% commission. Banks in small, remote places may still refuse to give a cash advance: try asking for the *gerente* (manager).

Opening hours

Generally Mon-Fri 0900-1800; closed for lunch some time between 1130 and 1400. **Shops** Also open on Sat until 1230 or 1300. **Government offices** Mon-Fri 1100-1800. **Banks** Mon-Fri 1000-1600 or 1630; closed at weekends.

Safety

Although Brazil's big cities suffer high rates of violent crime, this is mostly confined to the favelas (slums) where poverty and drugs are the main cause. Visitors should not enter favelas except when accompanied by workers for NGOs, tour groups or other people who know the local residents well and are accepted by the community. Otherwise they may be targets of muggings by armed gangs who show short shrift to those who resist them. Mugging can take place anywhere. Travel light after dark with few valuables (avoid wearing jewellery and use a cheap, plastic, digital watch). Ask hotel staff where is and isn't safe; crime is patchy in Brazilian cities.

If the worst does happen and you are threatened, don't panic, and hand over your valuables. Do not resist, and report the crime to the local tourist police later. It is extremely rare for a tourist to be hurt during a robbery in Brazil. Being aware of the dangers, acting confidently and using your common sense will reduce many of the risks.

Photocopy your passport, air ticket and other documents, make a record of traveller's cheque and credit card numbers. Keep them separately from the originals and leave another set of records at home. Keep all documents secure; hide your main cash supply in different places or under your clothes. Extra pockets sewn inside shirts and trousers, money belts (best worn below the waist), neck or leg pouches and elasticated support bandages for keeping money above the elbow or below the knee have been repeatedly recommended.

All border areas should be regarded with some caution because of smuggling activities. Violence over land ownership in parts of the interior have resulted in a 'Wild West' atmosphere in some towns, which should therefore be passed through quickly. Red-light districts should also be given a wide berth as there are reports of drinks being drugged with a substance popularly known as 'good night Cinderella'. This leaves the victim easily amenable to having their possessions stolen, or worse.

Avoiding cons

Never trust anyone telling sob stories or offering 'safe rooms', and when looking for a hotel, always choose the room yourself. Be wary of 'plain-clothes policemen'; insist on seeing identification and on going to the police station by main roads. Do not hand over your identification (or money) until you are at the station. On no account take them directly back to your hotel. Be even more suspicious if they seek confirmation of their status from a passer-by.

Hotel security

Hotel safe deposits are generally, but not always, secure. If you cannot get a receipt for valuables in a hotel safe, you can seal the contents in a plastic bag and sign across the seal. Always keep an inventory of what you have deposited. If you don't trust the hotel, lock everything in your pack and secure it in your room when you go out. If you lose valuables, report to the police and note details of the report for insurance purposes. Be sure to be present whenever your credit card is used.

Police

There are several types of police: **Polícia Federal**, civilian dressed, who handle all federal law duties, including immigration. A subdivision is the **Polícia Federal Rodoviária**, uniformed, who are the traffic police on federal highways. **Polícia Militar** are the uniformed, street police force, under the control of the state governor, handling all state laws. They are not the same as the Armed Forces' internal police. **Polícia Civil**, also state controlled, handle local laws and investigations. They are usually in civilian dress, unless in the traffic division. In cities, the **Prefeitura** controls the **Guarda Municipal**, who handle security. **Tourist police** operate in places with a strong tourist presence. In case of difficulty, visitors should seek out tourist police in the first instance.

Public transport

When you have all your luggage with you at a bus or railway station, be especially careful and carry any shoulder bags in front of you. To be extra safe, take a taxi between the airport/bus station/railway station and hotel, keep your bags with you and pay only when you and your luggage are outside; avoid night buses and arriving at your destination at night.

Time

Brazil has 4 time zones: Brazilian standard time is GMT-3; the Amazon time zone (Pará west of the Rio Xingu, Amazonas, Roraima, Rondônia, Mato Grosso and Mato Grosso do Sul) is GMT-4, the State of Acre is GMT-5; and the Fernando de Noronha archipelago is GMT-2. Clocks move forward 1 hr in summer for approximately 5 months (usually between Oct and Feb or Mar), but times of change vary. This does not apply to Acre.

Tipping

Tipping is not usual, but always appreciated as staff are often paid a pittance. In restaurants, add 10% of the bill if no service charge is included; cloakroom attendants deserve a small tip; porters have fixed charges but often receive tips as well; unofficial car parkers on city streets should be tipped 2 reais.

Tourist information

The **Ministério do Turismo**, Esplanada dos Ministérios, Bloco U, 2nd and 3rd floors, Brasília, www.turismo.gov.br or www.brazil tour.com, is in charge of tourism in Brazil and has information in many languages. **Embratur**, the Brazilian Institute of Tourism, is at the same address, and is in charge of promoting tourism abroad. For information and phone numbers for your country visit www.braziltour.com. Local tourist information bureaux are not usually helpful for information on cheap hotels – they generally just dish out pamphlets. Expensive hotels provide tourist magazines for their guests. Telephone directories (not Rio) contain good street maps.

Visas and immigration

Visas are not required for stays of up to 90 days by tourists from Andorra, Argentina, Austria, Bahamas, Barbados, Belgium, Bolivia, Chile, Colombia, Costa Rica, Denmark, Ecuador, Finland, France, Germany, Greece, Iceland, Ireland, Italy, Liechtenstein,

Luxembourg, Malaysia, Monaco, Morocco, Namibia, the Netherlands, Norway, Paraguay, Peru, Philippines, Portugal, San Marino, South Africa, Spain, Suriname, Sweden, Switzerland, Thailand, Trinidad and Tobago, United Kingdom, Uruguay, the Vatican and Venezuela. For them, only the following documents are required at the port of disembarkation: a passport valid for at least 6 months (or *cédula de identidad* for nationals of Argentina, Chile, Paraguay and Uruguay); and a return or onward ticket, or adequate proof that you can purchase your return fare, subject to no remuneration being received in Brazil and no legally binding or contractual documents being signed. Venezuelan passport holders can stay for 60 days on filling in a form at the border.

Citizens of the USA, Canada, Australia, New Zealand and other countries not mentioned above, and anyone wanting to stay longer than 180 days, *must* get a visa before arrival, which may, if you ask, be granted for multiple entry. US citizens must be fingerprinted on entry to Brazil. Visa fees vary from country to country, so apply to the Brazilian consulate in your home country. The consular fee in the USA is US$55. Students planning to study in Brazil or employees of foreign companies can apply for a 1- or 2-year visa. 2 copies of the application form, 2 photos, a letter from the sponsoring company or educational institution in Brazil, a police form showing no criminal convictions and a fee of around US$80 is required.

Weights and measures
Metric.

Contents

At a glance

Footprint features

⊖ **Getting around** Mostly by bus. Car hire recommended for the coast but not for the interior as roads can be poor.

⟳ **Time required** 2 days for Recife and Olinda, 3-5 days for the coast, 2-3 days for Fernando de Noronha.

❀ **Weather** Hot and wet summers (Mar-Jul), hot and drier winters (Sep-Feb).

✖ **When not to go** Apr and May are wet. Jun and Jul are wetter but are the best months for festivals.

Recife and around

Recife and around

Recife is one of the most attractive large cities in Brazil. From afar it looks as blighted by skyscrapers as Rio de Janiero or Belo Horizonte, but in the shadows are many fine colonial buildings from the sugar boom, watching over little shady squares or sitting on the edge of the filigree of canals and waterways that divide up the city. The colonial heart is Recife Antigo. This was a no-go area like Rio's Lapa until 15 years ago, but it's now the centre of the city's booming music and alternative culture scene. To the south of the centre are a string of urban beach suburbs – Pina, Boa Viagem and Piedade – which, although frequented by bull sharks, are among the cleanest urban beaches in the country (outside the busy weekends when locals leave rubbish on the sand). The city prides itself on good food and unique fashion and has many fine restaurants and boutiques. Although they retain separate names, Recife and Olinda have long ceased to be two cities. Olinda is now Recife's colonial suburb.

Many of Brazil's most famous contemporary avant-garde musicians are from Pernambuco, and Recife is considered Brazil's musical capital. Carnaval in the city of Recife and nearby Olinda is one of the best in the country. Nana Vasconcelos opens the festival leading a drum orchestra that dwarfs those in Bahia, and the maracatu prepares the way for three days of African-Brazilian cultural processions and relentless partying.

▶ *For listings, see pages 33-43.*

1 Recife orientation

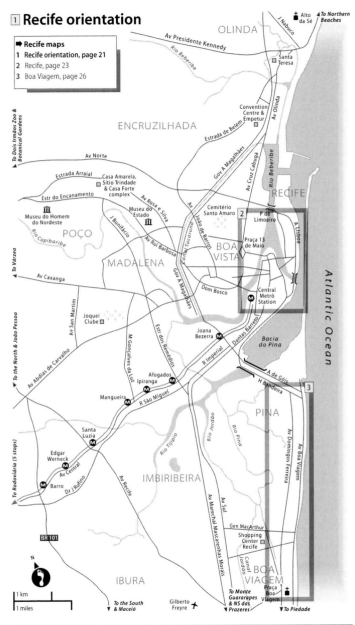

Ins and outs

Getting there International and domestic flights arrive at **Gilberto Freyre airport** ① *Guararapes, 12 km from the city centre, near the hotel district of Boa Viagem.* The airport is modern and spacious, with a tourist office, banks, shops, post office and car rental and tour agencies. Airport taxis cost US$5 to the seafront; bus No 52 runs to the centre, US$0.40.

Long-distance buses arrive at the **Terminal Integrado dos Passageiros (TIP)** ① *12 km outside the city near the Oficina Brenn and cultural museum at São Lourenço da Mata, T081-3452 1999,* pronounced 'chippy'. To get to the centre from the *rodoviária*, take the metrô to Central station, 30 minutes. If going to Boa Viagem, get off the metrô at Central station (Joanna Bezerra station is unsafe) and take a bus or taxi (US$8) from there. ▸▸ *See Transport, page 42.*

Getting around City buses cost US$0.90-1.50; they are clearly marked and run frequently until about 2230. Many central bus stops have boards showing routes. On buses, especially at night, look out for landmarks as street names are hard to see. Commuter services, known as the **metrô** but not underground, leave from the Central station; they have been extended to serve the *rodoviária* (frequent trains, 0500-2300, US$0.40 single). Integrated bus-metrô routes and tickets (US$1) are explained in a leaflet issued by **CBTU Metrorec,** T081-3251 5256. Trolleybuses run in the city centre. Taxis are plentiful; fares double on Sunday, after 2100 and during holidays.

Orientation The city centre consists of three sections sitting on islands formed by the rivers Capibaribe, Beberibe and Pina: **Recife Antigo**, **Santo Antônio** and **São José**. The inner city neighbourhoods of **Boa Vista** and **Santo Amaro** lie immediately behind to the east. The centre is always very busy by day; the crowds and narrow streets, especially in the Santo Antônio district, can make it a confusing city to walk around. But this adds to its charm. This is one of the few cities in Brazil where it is possible to get lost and chance upon a shady little square or imposing colonial church or mansion. Recife has the main dock area, with the commercial buildings associated with it. South of the centre is the residential and beach district of **Boa Viagem**, reached by bridge across the Bacia do Pina. **Olinda**, the old capital, is only 7 km to the north (see page 28). Although the streets are generally too full to present danger it is wise to be vigilant where the streets are quiet. Always take a taxi after dark if you are walking alone or in a pair.

Tourist information The main office for the Pernambuco tourist board, **Setur** ① *Centro de Convenções, Complexo Rodoviário de Salgadinho, Av Professor Andrade Bezerra s/n, Salgadinho, Olinda, T081-3182 8300, www.setur.pe.gov.br,* is between Recife and Olinda. There are other branches in Boa Viagem (T081-3463 3621), and at the airport (T081-3224 2361, open 24 hours); they cannot book hotels, but the helpful staff speak English and can offer leaflets and decent maps.

Safety Opportunistic theft is unfortunately common in the streets of Recife and Olinda (especially on the streets up to Alto da Sé). Keep a good hold on bags and cameras, and do not wear a watch. Prostitution is reportedly common in Boa Viagem, so choose nightclubs with care. Any problems contact the **tourist police** ① *T081- 3326 9603/ T081-3464 4088.*

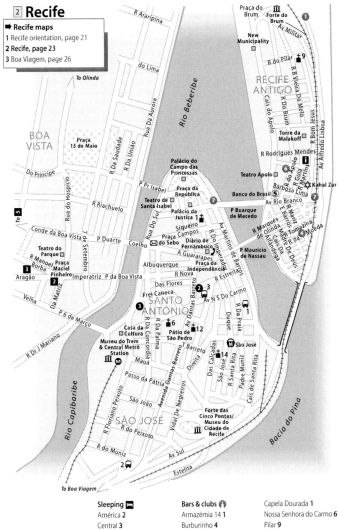

② Recife

➡ **Recife maps**

To Olinda

do Lima

R Araripina

do Princípe

BOA VISTA

Praça 13 de Maio

Rio Beberibe

Rio Capibaribe

R Da Aurora

R Da União

R Da Saudade

R Do Hospício

Rua do Hospício

R Riachuelo

Conde da Boa Vista

7 de Setembro

P Duarte

Coelho

Siqueiro

Teatro do Parque

R Manoel Borba

Praça Maciel Pinheiro

Aragão

Imperatriz

P da Boa Vista

Velha

Da Matriz

P 6 de Março

Frei Caneca

Das Flores

R Nova

Albuquerque

A Guararapes

Praça da Independência

Palácio do Campo das Princessas

P Pr Isabel

Praça da República

Teatro de Santa Isabel

Palácio da Justiça 1

Praça Campos

Diário de Pernambuco

R Do imperador

Do Sul

P Buarque de Macedo

P Maurício de Nassau

SANTO ANTÔNIO

R Da Concordia

R Da Palma

R Da Imperatriz

Av Dantas Barreto

Av N S Do Carmo

R Da Praia

Duque

Casa da Cultura

Pátio de São Pedro

São José

R Da Concordia

Museu do Trem & Central Metrô Station

Mauá

Passo da Pátria

São João

Avenida Dantas Barreto

Vidal De Negreiros

Direita

T Barreto

Das Calçadas

São José

R Santa Rita

Padre Muniz

Cais de Santa Rita

SÃO JOSÉ

R Floriano Peixoto

R Do Peixoto

R Do Muniz

Av Sul

Estelita

Forte das Cinco Pontas/ Museu do Cidade de Recife

Rio Capibaribe

Bacia do Pina

To Boa Viagem

Praça do Brum

Forte do Brum

New Municipality

Av Militar

R do Pilar 9

RB Vieira Do Mello

R Da Brum

R Do Melo

Cais do Apolo

RECIFE ANTIGO

Torre da Malakoff

R Rodrigues Mendes

Teatro Apolo

Banco do Brasil

Av Rio Branco

R Marques de Olinda

Kahal Zur

Barbosa Lima

R Da Moeda

Cais Do Apolo

Av Alfredo Lisboa

R Bom Jesus

R Martins Jr

Mãe Tomazina

Mãe De Deus

Madre De Deus

Alfândega

R J Mariano

To Itamaracá & Igarassu 1

To Porto das Galinhas 2

To Boa Viagem 3

N

200 metres
200 yards

Sights

Recife's architecture is far less celebrated than its pretty neighbour, the former Portuguese capital of Olinda, but it retains some very attractive buildings. Rua da Aurora, which watches over the Capibaribe river, is lined with stately palladian and neoclassical buildings. The islands to the south, over the filigree of bridges, are dotted with imposing churches and surprisingly lavish civic structures, especially around the Praça da República. The city began with the Dutch at the twin forts – the **Forte do Brum** on the island of **Recife Antigo** (Old Recife) which faces the open ocean, and the **Forte das Cinco Pontas** on the neighbouring island of Santo Antonio. Both were built by the Dutch in 1630, seven years before Maurice of Nassau sacked and burned Olinda. The two forts controlled access to the Dutch port of **Mauritsstadt**, as Recife was first known, at the northern and southern entrances respectively.

Recife Antigo This 2-km-long island, facing the open ocean on one side and the Rio Beberibe on the other, lays at the heart of old Recife. Until the 1990s its cobbled streets of handsome colonial buildings were a no-go area – frequented only by drug users and prostitutes. However, the area has been almost completely rehabilitated and Recife Antigo is now the spiritual heart of the city. The **Marco Zero** point, sitting in the Praça Rio Branco is the official centre of the city and the locus of activity for Recife's vibrant carnival. The best Pernambucan bands play on the stage here until dawn during carnival week and the streets nearby are busy with bars and little makeshift restaurants most evenings and especially at weekends. The liveliest street is Rua da Moeda.

The well-preserved whitewashed and terracotta-roofed **Forte do Brum** ① *Praça Comunidade Luso Brasileira s/n, T081-3224 8492, Tue-Fri 0900-1600, Sat and Sun 1300-1700, US$1* (1629), is now an army museum, with huge Dutch and Portuguese canons on its bulwarks, exhibition rooms with photographs and memorabilia from Brazil's Second Word War campaign in Italy and a dusty collection of colonial documents, including some early Dutch maps of Brazil. At the other end of Recife Antigo is the **Kahal Zur Israel Synagogue** ① *R do Bom Jesus 197, T081-3224 2128, Tue-Fri 1000-1200 and 1400-1700, US$2*, an exact replica of the first synagogue to be built in the Americas – in 1637. Under the Dutch, the 'New Christians' (Jews and Muslims forced to convert under the Inquisition), were given freedom to worship. After the city was re-conquered by the Portuguese the synagogue was destroyed and the Jews either fled or were expelled. Many went north to the Dutch colony of Suriname, which retains a large Jewish population to this day.

There are two other sights worth seeing in passing. One of the city's first churches, the elegant, sky-blue **Igreja de Nossa Senhora do Pilar** ① *R de São Jorge s/n*, dating from 1680 is undergoing extensive refurbishment after being badly looted and lying decrepit for decades. The intention is to return the crumbling church to its former glory, complete with its magnificent ceiling paintings. The **Torre** ① *Praça do Arsenal da Marinha, T082-3424 8704, Tue-Sun 1500-2000, free*, is a 19th-century mock-Mudejar tower with a small observatory on its upper floor. It's worth visiting if only for the sweeping view out over the city.

Santo Antônio and São José The bulk of Recife's historical monuments lie in the twin neighbourhoods of Santo Antônio and São José on the island immediately to the south of

Recife Antigo (and linked to that neighbourhood by the Buarque de Macedo and Mauricio de Nassau bridges). These neighbourhoods are interesting just to wander around (during the day only) and are replete with magnificent baroque churches. Most impressive of all is the **Capela Dourada da Ordem Terceira do São Francisco** ① *R do Imperador, Santo Antônio, T081-3224 0530, Mon-Fri and Sun 0800-1100 and 1400-1700* (1695-1710 and 19th century), in the church of Santo Antônio of the Convento do São Francisco. This is one of the finest baroque buildings in northeast Brazil and is another national monument. The lavish façade conceals a gorgeous gilt-painted interior with ceiling panels by Recife's Mestre Athayde, **Manuel de Jesus Pinto**. It is his finest work. Pinto was born a slave and bought his freedom after working on a series of Recife's magnificent churches, including the Concatedral de São Pedro dos Clérigos (see below). The chapel was designed and paid for in 1695 by a wealthy Franciscan lay brotherhood, the Ordem Terceira de São Francisco de Assis. The church sits immediately south of the **Praça da República**, one of the city's stateliest civic squares, graced by a fountain, shaded by palms and overlooked by a number of handsome sugar-boom buildings. These include the **Palácio do Campo das Princesas** ① *Praça da República s/n, Mon-Fri 0900-1700, free*, a neoclassical pile with a handsome interior garden by Roberto Burle Marx, which was formerly the Governor's Palace; the pink **Teatro de Santa Isabel** ① *Praça da República s/n, T081-3355 3323, www.teatrosanta isabel.com.br, guided visits Sun 1400 and 1700 in English, and almost nightly performances,* which has a lavish auditorium; and the imposing mock-French **Palácio da Justiça**, topped with a French Renaissance cupola.

Colonial Recife's other great church is the **Concatedral de São Pedro dos Clérigos** ① *Pátio de São Pedro, R Barão da Vitória at Av Dantas Barreto, T081-3224 2954, Mon-Fri 0800-1200 and 1400-1600*, which overlooks one of the city's best-preserved colonial squares, is only a little less impressive. It's a towering baroque building with a beautiful painted and carved octagonal interior with a trompe l'oeuil ceiling (also by Manuel de Jesus Pinto (see Capela Dourada, above). The area has been renovated and is filled with little shops, restaurants and bars. There are sporadic music and poetry shows in the evenings from Wednesday to Sunday. Also worth visiting is the 18th-century **Basílica e Convento de Nossa Senhora do Carmo** ① *Av Dantas Barreto, Santo Antônio, T081-3224 3341, Mon-Fri 0800-1200 and 1400-1900, Sat 0700-1200, Sun 0700-1000*, named after the city's patron saint, which has a magnificent painted ceiling and high altar. One of the best places in northeast Brazil to buy arts and crafts lies a stroll to the south, next to the Ponte 6 de Março. The **Casa da Cultura** ① *R Floriano Peixoto s/n, Santo Antônio, T081-3224 0557, www.casadaculturape.com.br, Mon-Fri 0900-1900, Sat 0900-1800, Sun 0900-1400*, is a gallery of hundreds of shops and stalls selling clay figurines, leatherwork, lace and ceramics from all over Pernambuco, including the famous arts and crafts town of Caruaru. The building is the former state penitentiary. Immediately west of the Casa da Cultura is Recife's other Dutch fort, the **Forte das Cinco Pontas**. This is now home to the **Museu da Cidade do Recife** ① *Mon-Fri 0900-1800, Sat and Sun 1300-1700, US$1 donation*, which shows a cartographic history of the settlement of Recife.

The **Basílica de Nossa Senhora de Penha** ① *Praça Dom Vital, São José, T081-3424 8500, Tue-Thu 0800-1200 and 1500-1700, Fri 0600-1800, Sat 1500-1700, Sun 0700-0900*, is an Italianate church a few streets north of the fort, which holds a traditional 'blessing of São Felix' on Fridays, attended by hundreds of sick Pernambucans in search of miracles.

3 Boa Viagem

To 1 & Recife Centre

Boa Viagem detail

➡ **Recife maps**
1 Recife orientation, page 21
2 Recife, page 23
3 **Boa Viagem, page 26**

Atlantic Ocean

N

200 metres
200 yards

Sleeping 🛏
Albergue do Mar 9
Aconchego 1
Coqueiral 2
Maracatú do Recife 3
Piratas de Praia 4
Pousada da Julieta 5
Pousada da Praia 6
Recife Monte 7
Uzi Praia 8
Vela Blanca 10

Eating 🍴
Borratcho 1
Chica Pitanga 2
Churrascaria Porção 3
É 4
Ilha da Kosta 5
La Capannina 6
La Maison 7
Parraxaxa 8
Peng 9
Real Eza 10
Romana 11
Soho 13
Tempero Verde 12

Suburban Recife

The **Oficina Brennand** ① *Propriedade Santos Cosme e Damião s/n, Várzea, T081-3271 2466, www.brennand.com.br, Mon-Fri 0800-1700, US$3*, is a Dali-esque fantasy garden and museum preserving hundreds of monumental ceramic sculptures by Latin America's most celebrated ceramic artist, Francisco Brennand. Enormous snake penises in hobnailed boots are set in verdant lawns; surrealist egret heads look out over a Burle Marx garden from 10-m-high tiled walls; haunting chess-piece figures in top hats gaze at tinkling fountains. The museum has a very good air-conditioned restaurant and gift shop. There is no public transport here so take a taxi from Recife (around US$15 including waiting time; alternatively take a local bus to the *rodoviária* or to Varzea suburb and do a round trip from there, US$10).

The Brennands are one of the wealthiest old-money families in Brazil and Ricardo Brennand – as if not to be outdone by his cousin – has his own museum 10 minutes' taxi ride away. The **Instituto Ricardo Brennand** ① *Alameda Antônio Brennand, Várzea, T081-2121 0352, www.institutoricardo brennand.org.br, Tue-Sun 1300-1700 (last entry 1630), US$3*, is a priceless collection of European and Brazilian art (including the largest conglomeration of Dutch-Brazilian landscapes in the world), books, manuscripts and medieval weapons housed in a fake Norman castle with its own moat and giant swimming pool.

Boa Viagem → *See map page 26.*

Recife's beach neighbourhood, and the site of most of the hotels, lies around 6 km south of town in the neighbourhood of Boa Viagem. The 8-km promenade lined with high-rise buildings commands a striking view of the Atlantic, but the beach is backed by a busy road, is crowded at weekends (when it is strewn with rubbish), and is plagued by bull sharks who lost their mangrove homes to the south after a spate of ill-considered coastal development. You can go fishing on *jangadas* at Boa Viagem at low tide. The main *praça* has a good market at weekends.

Ins and outs To get there from the centre, take any bus marked 'Boa Viagem'; from Nossa Senhora do Carmo, take buses marked 'Piedade', 'Candeias' or 'Aeroporto', which run along Avenida Domingos Ferreira, two blocks parallel to the beach, all the way to Praça Boa Viagem (at Avenida Boa Viagem 500). To get to the centre, take the bus marked 'CDU' or 'Setubal' from Avenida Domingos Ferreira. The PE-15 Boa Viagem to Olinda bus runs along the Avenida Boa Viagem and stops at the Praça Boa Viagem. It is fast and frequent.

Olinda → *For listings, see pages 33-43. Phone code: 081. Population: 350,000.*

About 7 km north of Recife is the old capital, a UNESCO World Heritage Site, founded in 1537. The compact network of cobbled streets is steeped in history and very inviting for a wander. Olinda is a charming spot to spend a few relaxing days, and a much more appealing base than Recife. A programme of restoration, partly financed by the Dutch government, was initiated in order to comply with the recently conferred title of 'national monument', but much is still in desperate need of repair.

Ins and outs

Getting there and around From Recife, take any bus marked 'Rio Doce', No 981, which has a circular route around the city and beaches; or No 33 from Avenida Nossa Senhora do Carmo, US$1.30; or 'Jardim Atlântico' from the central post office at Siqueira Campos (US$1.30, 30 minutes). From the airport, take the 'Aeroporto' bus to Avenida Domingos Ferreira in Boa Viagem and change to one of the buses mentioned above. From the Recife *rodoviária*, take the metrô to Central station (Joana Bezerra is unsafe) and then change. In all cases, alight in Olinda at Praça do Carmo. The PE-15 Boa Viagem bus runs between Olinda and Boa Viagem every 10-20 minutes (US$1.30, 20 minutes). Taxi drivers between Olinda and Recife often try to put their meters on rate 2 (only meant for Sundays, holidays and after 2100), but should change it to rate 1 when queried. A taxi from Boa Viagem should cost around US$14, US$20 at night. From Olinda to the centre of Recife, take a bus marked 'Piedade/Rio Doce' or 'Barra de Jangada/Casa Caiada'.

Tourist information The Secretaria de Turismo ① *Praça do Carmo, T081-3429 9279, daily 0900-2100*, provides a complete list of all historic sites and a useful map, *Sítio Histórico*. Guides with identification cards wait in Praça do Carmo. They are former street children and half the fee for a full tour of the city (about US$12) goes to a home for street children. If you take a guide you will be safe from mugging, which does unfortunately occur.

Sights

Whilst Olinda city boasts an ornate church on almost every corner, there are two which rank among the finest in South America – the Igreja e Convento Franciscano de Nossa Senhora das Neves (Brazil's first Franciscan convent) and the Basilica e Mosteiro de São Bento. The **Igreja e Convento Franciscano de Nossa Senhora das Neves** ① *Ladeira de São Francisco 280, T081-3429 0517, Mon-Fri 0700-1200 and 1400-1700, US$2, children free, mass Tue at 1900, Sat at 1700 and Sun at 0800*, (1585), is one of the oldest religious complexes in South America. It has a modest, weather-beaten exterior, but an interior that preserves one of the country's most splendid displays of woodcarving, ecclesiastical paintings and gilded stucco. The Franciscans began work on the buildings, which comprise the convent, the church of Nossa Senhora das Neves and the chapels of São Roque and St Anne, in 1585. Even if you are in a rush, be sure to visit the cloisters, the main church and the São Roque chapel, which is covered with beautiful Portuguese *azulejo* tiles.

The **Basilica e Mosteiro de São Bento** ① *R São Bento, T081-3429 3288, Mon-Fri 0830-1130, 1430-1700, Mass Sat 0630 and 1800; Sun 1000, with Gregorian chant; monastery closed except with written permission, free*, is another very early Brazilian church, founded in 1582 by Benedictine monks, burnt by the Dutch in 1631 and restored in 1761. It is the site of Brazil's first law school and was the first place in Brazil to abolish slavery. The vast, cavernous nave is fronted by a towering tropical cedar altarpiece covered in gilt. It is one of the finest pieces of baroque carving in the Americas and was on loan to the Guggenheim museum in New York for much of the first decade of the new millennium. There are fine carvings and paintings throughout the chapels.

It's worth making the short, but very steep, climb up the **Alto da Sé** to the plain and simple **Igreja da Sé** ① *Mon-Fri 0800-1200, 1400-1700* (1537), for the much- photographed views out over Olinda, the palm tree-fringed beaches and the distant skyscrapers of Recife. The chuch was the first to be built in Olinda and has been the city's cathedral since 1677. In the late afternoon and especially at weekends, there are often *repentista* street troubadours playing in the little cathedral square and women selling *tapioca* snacks. The **Igreja da Misericórdia** ① *R Bispo Coutinho, daily 1145-1230, 1800-1830* (1540), a short stroll downhill from the cathedral, has some beautiful *azulejo* tiling and gold work but seemingly random

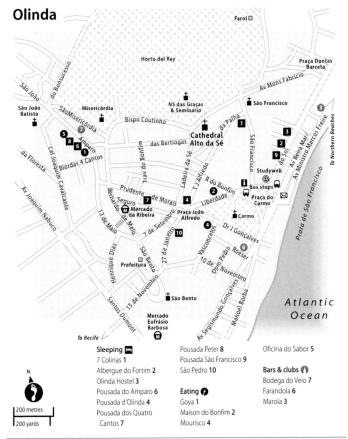

Olinda

Sleeping 🛌
7 Colinas 1
Albergue do Fortim 2
Olinda Hostel 3
Pousada do Amparo 6
Pousada d'Olinda 4
Pousada dos Quatro
  Cantos 7

Pousada Peter 8
Pousada São Francisco 9
São Pedro 10

Eating 🍴
Goya 1
Maison do Bonfim 2
Mourisco 4

Oficina do Sabor 5

Bars & clubs 🍸
Bodega do Veio 7
Farandola 6
Marola 3

opening hours. The **Igreja do Carmo** (1581), on a small hill overlooking Praça do Carmo, is similarly impressive, but has been closed for years despite assurances that it would be refurbished. Olinda has many handsome civic buildings too, including streets of 17th-century houses with latticed balconies, heavy doors and brightly painted stucco walls. Some, like the mansion housing the **Mourisco** restaurant (Praça João Alfredo 7), are in the Portuguese Manueline style, their façades replete with Moorish architectural motifs.

There's a thriving arts and crafts community in Olinda and this is a good place to stock up on regional souvenirs. Look out for terracotta figurines and woodcarvings. The figurines are often by named artisans (look for their autograph imprinted in the clay on the base) and are becoming collectors' items. You'll find shops selling arts and crafts near the cathedral and in the handicraft shops at the **Mercado da Ribeira** ① *R Bernardo Vieira de Melo*, and the **Mercado Eufrásio Barbosa** ① *Av Segismundo Gonçalves at Santos Dumont, Varadouro*. Every Friday at 2200 there are serenades in Olinda, with a troupe of musicians leaving the Praça João Alfredo (aka Praça da Abolição) and walking throughout the old centre.

The beaches close to Olinda are polluted, but those further north, beyond Casa Caiada, at **Janga**, and **Pau Amarelo**, are beautiful, palm-fringed and usually deserted (although the latter can be dirty at low tide). There are many simple cafés where you can eat *sururu* (clam stew in coconut sauce), *agulha frita* (fried needle-fish), *miúdo de galinha* (chicken giblets in gravy), *casquinha de carangueijo* (seasoned crabmeat) and *farinha de dendê* (served in crab shells). Visit the Dutch fort on Pau Amarelo beach where there is a small craft fair on Saturday nights. To get to the beaches, take either a 'Janga' or 'Pau Amarela' bus; to return to Recife, take a bus marked 'Varodouro'.

Southern coast → *For listings, see pages 33-43.*

Gaibú and around

Heading south from Recife are some of the best beaches in the state. The first stop is the beautiful and quiet beach at **Gaibú**, 30 km south, where there are *pousadas* and cheap restaurants. The scenic **Cabo de Santo Agostinho**, with a ruined fort, is 5 km to the east. About 1 km on foot from Gaibú is the beautiful **Praia Calhetas**. The beach at **Itapuama** is even emptier. Buses to Gaibú and the beaches run frequently from **Cabo**, Pernambuco's main industrial city, which has a few interesting churches and forts and a **Museu da Abolição**, which has dusty displays about the history and abolition of the slave trade. To get to Cabo take a bus signed 'Centro do Cabo' from the airport in Recife.

Nearby, **Suape** has many 17th-century buildings, while the **Reserva Biológica de Saltinho**, www.museudouna.com.br/saltinho.htm, preserves some of the last vestiges of Atlantic forest in the northeast.

Porto de Galinhas → *Phone code: 081.*

Some 60 km south of Recife, Porto de Galinhas – whose name means 'port of chickens' because slaves were smuggled here in chicken crates – was one of the first of a string of low-key beach resorts discovered in the 1990s. Back then it was little more than a beach and two sandy streets; the myth of its tranquil charm endures – but it is only a myth. Today Porto de Galinhas is well on its way to becoming a full-scale resort comparable those near Porto Seguro in Bahia. The sandy streets are asphalted and lined with shops and restaurants, while the beaches are backed with *pousadas* and resort hotels for several kilometres north and south. There is a reef close to the shore, so swimming is only possible at high tide.

Buses and minivans run from Avenida Dantas Barreto and Rua do Peixoto in Recife, at least hourly. Taxis cost around US$50. The Centro de Informacões Turísticas ① *R da Esperança s/n, T081-3552 1728, www.bureaudeinformacoes.tur.br*, has maps, information on transport, hotels and tour operators and a few English-speaking staff.

South of Porto de Galinhas

Some 80 km south of Recife are the beaches of **Barra do Sirinhaém**, with some tourist development and three hotels, including **Dos Catavventos** (**D**). Fishermen make trips to offshore islands (good views). Beyond these are the little towns of **Tamandare** and **São José da Coroa Grande**, which are quieter than Porto de Galinhas, and have a few simple places to stay.

Northern coast → *For listings, see pages 33-43.*

Igarassu → *Phone code: 081. Population: 77,500.*

Some 39 km north of Recife on the road to João Pessoa, Igarassu has the first church built in Brazil, **SS Cosme e Damião** (1535) and the convent of **Santo Antônio**, a beautiful baroque building with some very fine gilt work and *azulejos*.

Itamaracá → *Phone code: 081. Population: 14,000.*

North of Igarassu the road passes through coconut plantations to **Itapissuma**, where there is a bridge to **Itamaracá** island. According to the locals, this is where Adam and Eve spent their holidays (so does everyone else on Sunday now). It has the old Dutch **Forte Orange**, built in 1631; an interesting penal settlement with gift shops, built round the 1747 sugar estate buildings of Engenho São João, which still have much of the old machinery, charming villages and colonial churches, as well as some fine, wide beaches. At one of them, **Praia do Forte Orange**, the Instituto Chico Mendes de Conservação da Biodiversidade (ICMBio) has a centre for the study and preservation of manatees, **Centro Nacional de Conservação e Manejo de Sirênios** or Peixe-boi ① *Tue-Sun 1000-1600.*

There are pleasant trips by *jangada* from Praia do Forte Orange to **Ilha Coroa do Avião**, a recently formed sandy island, which has rustic beach bars and a research station for the development of wildlife and migratory birds. The beaches of **Sossego** and **Enseada** also have some bars but are quiet and relatively undiscovered. The crossing is 3 km north of Itamaracá town; recommended for sun worshippers.

Further north again, two hours from Recife by bus, is **Pontas de Pedra**, an old fishing village with a nice beach, lots of bars and opportunities for fishing and diving.

At the Pernambuco–Paraíba border, a 27-km dirt road goes to the fishing village of **Pitimbu**, with *jangadas*, surf fishing, lobster fishing and lobster-pot making. There are no tourist facilities but camping is possible and food is available from **Bar do Jangadeiro**. To get here, take a bus from Goiana, US$1.

West of Recife → *For listings, see pages 33-43.*

Bezerros → *Phone code: 081. Population: 52,000.*

The town of Bezerros, 15 km west of Recife on the BR-232, is set next to the Rio Ipojuca. It has some old houses, fine *praças* and churches. Some, like the **Igreja de Nossa Senhora dos Homens Pretos**, **São José** and the **Capela de Nossa Senhora**, date from the 19th century. The former railway station has been converted into the **Estação da Cultura**, with shows and other cultural performances. The best known artist and poet is José Borges (born 1935), whose work has been exhibited internationally. The city's main attraction is handicrafts, which are found in the district of **Encruzilhada de São João**. Most typical are the Papangu masks, made of painted papier mâché, and used at Carnaval as interior decoration. Wooden toys are also popular, as well as items made from leather and clay. About 10 km from the centre of Bezerros, near the village of Serra Negra, a small eco-tourism park, **Serra Negra ecological tourism trail**, has been set up. Trails lead to caves and springs; the flora is typical of the *agreste*.

Carnaval here is famed throughout Brazil and is known as **Folia do Papangu**, see Festivals, page 39. For tourist information contact the **Departamento de Turismo** ① *Praça Duque de Caxias 88, Centro, T081-3328 1286*. The artisans association, **Associação dos Artesãos de Bezerros**, is at the same address.

Caruaru → *Phone code: 081. Population: 254,000. Altitude: 554 m.*

Situated 134 km west of Recife, this small town in the *sertão* is famous for its huge **Festas Juninas**, held throughout June (see Festivals and events, page 39), and its little clay figures (*figurinhas* or *bonecas de barro*) originated by Mestre Vitalino (1909-1963), and very typical of northeast Brazil. Most of the potters live at **Alto da Moura**, 6 km away, where you can visit the **Casa Museu Mestre Vitalino** ① *buses from Caruaru, a bumpy 30-min ride, US$0.50*, once owned by Vitalino and containing personal objects and photographs, but no examples of his work. UNESCO has recognized the area as the largest centre of figurative art in the Americas. It is also possible to buy the arts and crafts in Caruaru itself. The town hosts a number of markets, which were originally devoted to foodstuffs but which now also sell arts and crafts. The most famous is the **Feira da Sulanca**, held in the city centre on Tuesdays, with some 10,000 stalls and 40,000 visitors.

Ins and outs The *rodoviária* is 4 km west of town; buses from Recife stop in the town centre. Alight here and look for the **Livraria Estudantil**, on the corner of Vigário Freire and Rua Anna de Albuquerque Galvão; this is a useful landmark. Follow Galvão down hill from the bookshop, turn right on Rua 15 de Novembro to the first junction, 13 de Maio; turn left, and finally cross the river to the Feira do Artesanato (arts and crafts market).

During the Festas Juninas, there is a tourist train, **Train do Forró**, from Recife, which is a very spirited affair with bars, and bands playing in the carriages. See www.tremdo forro.com.br and www.caruaru.pe.gov.br for information.

Fazenda Nova and Nova Jerusalém

During Easter Week each year, various agencies run package tours to the little country town of Fazenda Nova, 23 km from Caruaru. Just outside the town is Nova Jerusalém. Every day from the day before Palm Sunday up to Easter Saturday, an annual Passion play is enacted here, on an open-air site about one third the size of the historic quarter of Jerusalem. Nine stages are used to depict scenes from the Passion of Christ, which is presented using 50 actors and 500 extras to re-enact the story with the audience following in their footsteps. *TV Globo* stars often play the starring roles and the sound and lighting effects are state of the art. Performances begin at 1800 and last for about three hours.

There is little accommodation in Nova Jerusalém/Fazenda Nova and it is usually full during the Passion. **Empetur** in Recife/Olinda has details of agencies that offer trips. During the Easter period there are direct bus services from Recife (and from Caruaru at other times).

Recife and around listings

For Sleeping and Eating price codes and other relevant information, see page 8-11.

🛏 Sleeping

Recife *p20, maps p21 and p23*
For the city centre, the best pace to stay is **Boa Vista**. Be careful walking back to hotels after dark. During **Carnaval** and for longer stays, individuals rent private rooms and houses in Recife and Olinda; listings can be found in the classified ads of *Diário de Pernambuco*. This accommodation is generally cheaper, safer and quieter than hotels.

$$$ Pousada Villa Boa Vista, R Miguel Couto 81, Boa Vista, T081-3223 0666, www.pousada villaboavista.com.br. The only modern hotel in town, with plain, comfortable a/c rooms (all en suites have modern bathrooms and powerful showers), around a courtyard. Quiet, safe and a 5-min taxi ride from the centre.

$ América, Praça Maciel Pinheiro 48, Boa Vista, T081-3423 2707, www.hotelamerica recife.com.br. Frayed, very simple rooms with low, foamy beds, lino floors and tiny en suites. The best rooms are on the upper floors with views out over the city.

$ Central, Av Manoel Borba 209, Boa Vista, T081-3222 2353. A splendid 1920s building with its original French open lifts and plain, but freshly painted rooms with parquet flooring and flat-pack furniture. The bathrooms have enormous iron tubs (without plugs). The upper floors have wonderful views of the city.

Boa Viagem *p27, map p26*
Boa Viagem is the main tourist district and although it has plenty of hotels it is a long way from the centre of Recife. The beach is notorious for shark attacks. The main beachfront road is **Av Boa Viagem**; hotels here are mostly tower blocks and tend to be more expensive.

$$ Aconchego, Félix de Brito 382, T081-3464 2960, www.hotelaconchego.com.br. Motel-style rooms around a pleasant pool area, a/c, sitting room. English-speaking owner, will collect you from the airport.

$$ Coqueiral, R Petrolina, 43, T081-3326 5881, www.hotelcoqueiral.com.br. Dutch-owned (English and French spoken). Small, homely rooms with a/c and a pretty breakfast room. Recommended.

$$ Pousada da Praia, Alcides Carneiro Leal 66, T081-3326 7085, www.hpraia.com. This ungainly blue block 50 m from the beach has very simple tiled rooms – some pocket-sized and with little more than a spongey bed, others larger suites with space for up to 6. All are a/c and come with a TV, safe and Wi-Fi and there is a rooftop breakfast and lounge area.

$$ Recife Monte, on the corner of R Petrolina and R dos Navegantes 363, T081-2121 0909, www.recifemontehotel.com.br. A big tower with 150 rooms and a string of smarter duplex suites watching over a gloomy atrium with a small shaded pool, Rooms are good value for the category and the crowd are predominantly business travellers.

$ Piratas da Praia, Av Conselheiro Aguiar 2034, 3rd floor, T081-3326 1281, www.piratas dapraia.com. This popular hostel sits close to bakeries, *botecos* and a number of bars and block back from the beach. Fan-cooled rooms and dorms are colourful but a little pokey, but pleasant public areas include a living area with rather uncomfortable plastic seats and a well-appointed kitchen. Staff speak some English can organize trips and give local travel advice, and there is free Wi-Fi.

$ Pousada da Julieta, R Prof José Brandao 135, T081-3326 7860, hjulieta@elogica.com.br. Friendly and clean. One block from beach, very good value. Recommended.

Olinda *p28, map p29*

Travellers generally tend to use Olinda as a base rather than Recife as it is safer, prettier and its sights, restaurants and bars are concentrated in a relatively small area. Transport to Recife is straightforward (see page 42). Prices at least triple during Carnaval when 5-night packages are sold. Rooms at regular prices can often be found in Boa Viagem during this time. In the historic centre, accommodation is mostly in converted mansions, which are full of character. If you can afford it, staying in one of these *pousadas* is the ideal way to absorb Olinda's colonial charm. All *pousadas*, and most of the cheaper hotels outside the old city, have a pool.

$$$ 7 Colinas, Ladeira de Sao Francisco 307, T/F081-3439 7766, www.hotel7colinas. com.br. Spacious, new hotel with all mod cons, set in private, gated gardens and with a large swimming pool.

$$$ Pousada do Amparo, R do Amparo 199, T081-3439 1749, www.pousadadoamparo. com.br. Olinda's best hotel is a gorgeous, 18th-century house, full of antiques and atmosphere in the **Roteiros do Charme** group (see page 10). Rooms have 4-poster beds and each is decorated differently. The public areas include a spacious foyer with a high ceiling decorated with art, a pool and sauna area surrounded by a little flower- filled garden and an excellent, delightfully romantic restaurant.

$$ Olinda Hostel, R do Sol 233, T081- 3429 1592, www.alberguedeolinda.com.br. HI youth hostel with fan-cooled 8-bed dorms with shared en suites, and doubles. The hostel has a tropical garden, TV room, and a shady area with hammocks next to a pool.

$$ Pousada d'Olinda, P João Alfredo 178, T/F081-3494 2559, www.pousadadolinda. com.br. Basic but well-kept dorms and doubles around a pool, garden and communal breakfast area and lunchtime restaurant. Discount of 10% for owners of **Footprint** guides. English, French, German Arabic and Spanish spoken.

$$ Pousada dos Quatro Cantos, R Prudente de Morais 441, T081-3429 0220, www.pousada4 cantos.com.br. A large converted townhouse with a little walled garden and terraces. The maze of bright rooms and suites are decorated with Pernambuco arts and crafts and furnished mostly with antiques. Warm, welcoming and full of character.

$$ Pousada Peter, R do Amparo 215, T081- 3439 2171, www.pousadapeter.com.br. The rather pokey white-tiled a/c rooms in this converted town house contrast with the spacious lobby lounge decorated with Pernambuco crafts and colourful artwork. Breakfast is served on the terrace overlooking distant Recife and the modest pool.

$$ Pousada São Francisco, R do Sol 127, T081-3429 2109, www.pousadasao francisco.com.br. Well-kept and airy a/c rooms with little terraces, slate floors and pokey bathrooms housed in a modern 2-storey hotel overlooking a pool and bar area and set in pleasant gardens, which are visited by hummingbirds in the early morning. The hotel has a small restaurant and parking. Outside the historic centre but within walking distance.

$ São Pedro, R 27 Janeiro 95, T081-3439

9546, www.pousadapedro.com. Quiet little *pousada* with a walled garden, a small pool shaded by frangipani and bamboo. Has a delightful breakfast area and lobby decorated with art and antiques. The rustic rooms are tiny but tastefully decorated and all a/c. The best are on the upper floor.

$ Pousada do Fortim, R do Sol 151, T081-3439 7124, www.pousadadofortim.com.br. Very simple but clean boxy rooms with a/c at the cheapest rates in Olinda. Some are big enough for 4. Breakfast is US$2 extra.

Camping
Olinda Camping, R Bom Sucesso 262, Amparo, T081-3429 1365. US$5 per person, space for 30 tents, 5 trailers, small huts for rent, quiet, well-shaded, town buses pass outside. Recommended.

Gaibú *p30*
$$$$ Casa dos Golfinhos, Gaibu beach, T081- 8861 4707, www.gaibu-bedandbreakfast.com. Bed and breakfast accommodation close to the beach, under German management.

Porto de Galinhas *p30*
There are plenty of cheap *pousadas* and hotels in town along **R da Esperança** and its continuation **R Manoel Uchôa**; also along **R Beijapurá**, which runs off R da Esperança.
$$$$ Village Porto de Galinhas, T081-3552 2945, www.villageportodegalinhas.com.br. All-inclusive family beach resort right on the ocean and with a large pool, restaurant, a/c rooms. Some 7 km from town.
$$ HI Pousada A Casa Branca, Praça 18, T081-3552 1808, www.pousadaacasabranca.com.br. Very clean, well-kept, newly opened hostel with some a/c rooms and several dorms. To get there take the right turn (away from the sea) off R Beijupira opposite R Carauna and walk inland for 400 m. The *pousada* is in a little

square 150 m before the Estrada Maracaipe.
$$ La Vila delle Rose, R Manoel Uchôa 11, T081-3552 1489, www.laviladellerose.com.br. Simple, bright and well-kept doubles and shared rooms in a large house very close to the beach. Good breakfast and friendly service. All en suites.

Igarassu *p31*
Camping
Engenho Monjope, 5 km before Igarassu coming from Recife, T081-3543 0528, US$5. A Camping Clube do Brasil site on an old sugar estate, now a historical monument (bus US$1, alight at the 'Camping' sign and walk 5-10 mins).

Itamaracá *p31*
$$ Casa da Praia, Av da Forte Orange, T081-3544 1255. With pool, minibar, breakfast and optional dinner.
$$ Pousada Itamaracá, R Fernando Lopes 205/210, T081-3544 1152, www.pousadadeitamaraca.com.br. Away from the beach, but has a pool.

Caruaru *p32*
A large number of cheap *hospedarias* can be found around the central square, Praça Getúlio Vargas.
$$$ Grande Hotel São Vicente de Paulo, Av Rio Branco 365, T081-3721 5011, www.grandehotel caruaru.com.br. A good, centrally located hotel with a/c, laundry, garage, bar, restaurant, pool, TV. It also houses the local cinema.
$$ Centenário, 7 de Setembro 84, T081-3722 4011. Also has more expensive suites and a pool. The breakfast is good. As the hotel is in the town centre it can be noisy, but otherwise recommended.
$$ Central, R Vigario Freire 71, T081-3721 5880. Suites or rooms, all with a/c, TV, good breakfast, in the centre. Recommended.

🍴 Eating

Recife *p20, maps p21 and p23*

The best Recife restaurants are in **Boa Viagem** (see below) and adjacent Pina. Be careful of eating the local crabs, known as *guaiamum*; they live in the mangrove swamps which take the drainage from Recife's *mocambos* (shanty towns).

There are many cheap *lanchonetes* catering to office workers, they are shut in evening.

ⵉⵉⵉ Leite, Praça Joaquim Nabuco 147/53 near the Casa de Cultura, Santo Antônio. This formal Portuguese-Brazilian fusion restaurant, with black-tie waiters and a live pianist, is one of the oldest in the country and has been serving Portuguese standards like bacalhau (smoked salted cod) for 120 years. More modern options on the 50+ dish menu include king prawns fried in garlic butter and served with cream cheese sauce and Brazil nut rice. It is frequently voted the best in the city.

ⵉ Gellatos, Av Dantas Barreto, 230. Great juices (*sucos*) – try the delicious *guarana do amazonas* with nuts. Snacks include, hamburgers and sandwiches.

Boa Viagem *p27, map p26*

Restaurants on the main beach road of **Av Boa Viagem** are pricier than in the centre. Venture a block or 2 inland for cheaper deals. There are many a/c cheapies in the **Shopping Center Recife**, T081-3464 6000. Many of the better restaurants are closed on Mon.

ⵉⵉⵉ Churrascaria Porção, R Ernesto de Paula Santos 1368, T081-3465 3999, www.porcao. com.br. This widespread upmarket Brazilian *churrascaria* chain is good for meat- and salad-eaters alike – with a huge salad and pasta bar as well as the usual waiters whisking sizzling spit roast cuts of meat from the kitchen.

ⵉⵉⵉ É Gastronomia, R do Atlantico 147, Pina, T081-3225 9323, www.egastronomia.com.br. Warm reds, mirrors, low light, candles on the table and chill out music make this recent

opening feel like a lounge room in a swish London club. Chef Douglas Van Der Ley serves classic French dishes with a Brazilian twist, with plates like fillet steak with foie gras, accompanied with sweet potato puree and cheese tartlet. The dessert menu changes daily.

ⵉⵉⵉ La Maison, Av Boa Viagem, 618, T081-3325 1158. This fondue restaurant in a low- lit basement has an illicit dive bar feel and cheesy 1970s decor, but its good fun, attracts a lively crowd and has stodgy desserts like peach melba on the menu.

ⵉⵉ Chica Pitanga, R Petrolina, 19, T081-3465 2224. Upmarket, excellent food by weight. Be prepared to queue. Recommended.

ⵉⵉ Ilha da Kosta, R Pe Bernardino Pessoa 50, T081-3466 2222, www.ilhadakosta.com.br. One of half a dozen good-value restaurants serving everything from steaks and Bahian stews to sushi and roast chicken. These sit alongside a variety of *petisco* snacks. Open from 1100 until the last client leaves.

ⵉⵉ La Capannina, Av Cons Aguiar 538, T081-3465 9420. Italian pizzas, salad, pasta and sweet and savoury crêpes. Recommended.

ⵉⵉ Parraxaxa, R Baltazar Pereira, 32, T081-3463 7874, www.parraxaxa.com.br. Rustic-style, award-winning buffet of north-eastern cuisine, with tapioca breakfasts and a generous spread of dishes at lunch and dinner time. The dining room is decorated with effigies of the *sertão* bandit Lampião and his consort Maria Bonita.

ⵉ Peng, Av Eng Domingos Ferreira, 2886, T081-3326 9149. Self-service, some Chinese dishes. Bargain, rather than gourmet food.

ⵉ Tempero Verde, R SH, Cardim, opposite **Chica Pitanga**. Where the locals go for a bargain meal of beans, meat and salad, US1.50. Simple, self-service, street tables.

ⵉ TioDadá, R Baltazar Pereira, 100. Loud, TV screens, good-value portions of beef.

Olinda *p28, map p29*

Try *tapioca*, a local dish made of manioc with coconut or cheese. The traditional Olinda drinks, *pau do índio* (with 32 herbs) and *retetel* are manufactured on R do Amparo.

There are a number of *lanchonetes* and fast-food options along the seafront, including **Mama Luise** and **Gibi**, Av Min Marcos Freire, and **Leque Moleque**, Av Sigismundo Gonçalves 537.

⫙⫙⫙ Goya, R do Amparo 157, T081- 3439 4875. Regional food, particularly seafood, beautifully presented.

⫙⫙⫙ Oficina do Sabor, R do Amparo 355, T081-3429 3331. Chef Cesar Santos runs the kitchen at what is probably the city's best restaurant, serving traditional Lusitanian dishes like Portuguese *bacalhau* (salted codfish) and surubim catfish in passionfruit soubise with sautéed sweet potato and rice. Tables sit in a colourful dining room and on an al fresco terrace with sea views. There are plenty of vegetarian options.

⫙⫙ Maison do Bonfim, R do Bonfim 115, T081-3429 1674. English-trained chef Jeff Colas serves a choice of European dishes like mini vol-au-vent de Roquefort and *carpaccio com rúcula e tomate seco e mostarda francesa* (carpaccio with rocket and sun-dried tomato with French mustard) in this attractive Portuguese town house on the most elegant colonial street in the city. The wine list is one of the best in Olinda, with a choice of Argentine and Chilean reds.

⫙⫙ Samburá, Av Min Marcos Freire 1551. With terrace, try *caldeirada* and *pitu* (crayfish), also lobster in coconut sauce or daily fish dishes, very good.

⫙ Grande Pequim, Av Min Marcos Freire 1463, Bairro Novo. Good Chinese food.

⫙ Mourisco, Praça João Alfredo. Excellent, good-value food by weight in lovely, part-covered garden. Delicious deserts. A real find. Warmly recommended.

Caruaru *p32*
Alto da Moura is a real tourist spot and gets very busy.

⫙-⫙ Catracho's, close to São Sebastião hospital. Has a Caribbean feel and the Honduran owner mixes great cocktails.

⫙-⫙ Costela do Baiano, close to Igreja do Rosário. Very good value northeastern cooking with good seafood.

⫙ A Massa, R Vidal de Negreiros. The best of a number of cheap lunch restaurants in the centre near Banco do Brasil. With respectable pizzas and pasta.

🎶 Bars and clubs

Recife *p20, maps p21 and p23*
Recife and Olinda are reknowned for their lively nightlife. There is frequent live music – both in public spaces and in Recife and Olinda's numerous theatres. The website http://bacurau.com.br has details of what's on where.

Recife Antigo is the best place in the city for weekend nightlife. Many exciting bands post mangue beat fusion bands and DJs play in the bars and clubs around **R Tomazino** (R do Burburinho); and there is always a lively crowd. The area is not safe to walk to so take a taxi. The best listings site is www.reciferock.com.br and has information on live post-mangue beat music.

Armazém 14, Av Alfredo Lisboa s/n, Cais do Porto, Recife Antigo. One of the top live music venues for the alternative scene. Big names like Mundo Livre and Mombojo play here.

Boratcho, Galeria Joana Darc, Pina, T081-3327 1168. Tex Mex restaurant and live music venue for alternative *mangue beat* bands. Alternative and gay crowd.

Burburinho, R Tomazina 106, T081-3224 5854. The best of the live music spots in Recife Antigo. Grungy, arty crowd and a range of sounds from psychedelic *forró* funk to *frevo* rock and all things mixed. Other bars lie near by – start here and wander.

Central, R Mamede Simões 144, Boa Vista, T081-3222 7622, www.centralrecife.com.br. The drinking hole of choice for the city's

Naná Vasconcelos

Brazilian music without Recife's master percussionist Naná Vasconcelos would be like jazz without Charles Mingus. Bossa nova had been introduced into the USA by Stan Getz. But it was Naná and Paranense Airto Moreira who placed Brazilian percussion in the upper echelons of the serious jazz world. Naná was introduced to the US jazz scene by Miles Davis who went to one of the percussionist's concerts in the 1970s. And during a 25-year sojourn in New York he added his trademark *berimbau* and percussion to scores of records by artists like the CODONA trio (which he led with Don Cherry and Colin Walcott), Jan Garbarek, Pat Metheny, Gato Barbieri and numerous others. His most remarkable work, though, is purely Brazilian. Together with Egberto Gismonti and on albums like *Dança das Cabecas* (ECM), he created a new musical genre which fused jazz, classical and Brazilian styles. And his *Fragmentos* (Nucleo Contemporaneo/Tzadik) and *Storytelling* (EMI) albums are complex, mesmerizing tapestries of percussion and vocals that beautifully evoke Brazilian landscapes and local people.

musical and artistic middle-class community. Decent bar food, lunches and breakfast.
Depois Dancing Bar, Av Rio Branco 66, T081-3424 7451. Well-established alternative dance club with live bands.
Estação Pirata, R do Apolo, Recife Antigo. Good live bands – look out for Eddie and Tine who play here.

***

Olinda *p28, map p29*
Beginning at dusk, but best after 2100, the **Alto da Sé** becomes the scene of a small street fair, with arts, crafts, makeshift bars, barbecue stands, and impromptu traditional music. Every Fri night band musicians walk the streets serenading passers-by. Each Sun from 1 Jan to Carnaval there is a mini carnival in the streets of the city, with live music and dancing.
Bodega do Veio, R do Amparo 212, T081-3429 0185. An Olinda institution with live music Thu-Sun. Sat nights are hosted by a famous local fiddle player, Mestre Saluciano, and his band, who play traditional *pe na serra forró*. Great *petiscos* (especially the *prato frio*) and caipirinhas.
Cantinho da Sé, Ladeira da Sé 305, T081-

3439 8815. Lively, good view of Recife, food served.
Farandola, R Dom Pedro Roeser, 190, tucked away behind Igreja do Carmo church. Mellow bar with festival theme and big top-style roof. Live music nightly, plans for a circus next door. Drinks are cheap; try *bate bate de maracuja* (smooth blend of *cachaça*, passionfruit juice and honey) or *raspa raspa* fruit syrup. Warmly recommended.
Marola, Tr Av Dantas Barreto 66, T081-3429 2499. Funky wooden *barraca* on rocky shore-line specializing in seafood. Great *caiprifrutas* (frozen fruit drink with vodka). Can get crowded. Recommended.
Pernambucanamente, Av Min Marcos Freire 734, Bairro Novo, T081-3429 1977. Live, local music every night.

***

Itamaracá *p31*
Bar da Lia, R do Jaguaribe, close to the Forte Orange, weekends feature *cirandas* danced at the bar, led by the well-known singer, Dona Lia, and her band. Also serves food. In high season only – from Sep to after carnival.

Recife *p20, maps p21 and p23*
For **Carnaval**, see box, next page.
1 Jan Universal Brotherhood.
12-15 Mar Parades to mark the city's foundation.
Mid-Apr Pro-Rock Festival, a week-long celebration of rock, hip-hop and *mangue beat* SP at Centro de Convenções, Complexo de Salgadinho and other venues. Check *Diário de Pernambuco* or *Jornal de Comércio* for details.
Jun Festas Juninas, see box, page 75.
11-16 Jul Nossa Senhora do Carmo, patron saint of the city.
Aug Mes do Folclore.
1-8 Dec Festival of Lemanjá, with typical foods and drinks, celebrations and offerings to the goddess.
8 Dec Nossa Senhora da Conceição.

Olinda *p28, map p29*
Feb Carnaval. Thousands of people dance through the narrow streets of the old city to the sound of the *frevo*, the brash energetic music that normally accompanies a lively dance performed with umbrellas. The local people decorate them with streamers and straw dolls, and form themselves into costumed groups (*blocos*), which you can join as they pass (take only essentials). Among the best-known *blocos*, which carry life-size dolls, are **O homem da meianoite** (Midnight Man), **A Corda** (a pun on 'the rope' and 'acorda' – wake up!), which parades in the early hours, **Pitombeira** and **Elefantes**. Olinda's carnival continues on Ash Wed, but is much more low-key, *a quarta-feira do batata* (Potato Wednesday, named after a waiter who claimed his right to celebrate Carnaval after being on duty during the official celebrations). The streets are very crowded with people dancing and drinking non-stop. The local cocktail, *capeta* (guaraná powder, sweet skimmed milk and vodka) is designed to keep you going.

12-15 Mar Foundation Day, 3 days of music and dancing, night-time only.

Bezerros *p32*
Feb Carnaval celebrations are famous throughout Brazil and known as **Folia do Papangu**. Papangu characters wear masks that resemble a cross between a bear and a devil and are covered from head to foot in a costume like a bear skin (or an all-covering white tunic).
Jun São João.

Caruaru *p32*
Mar/Apr Semana Santa, Holy Week, with lots of folklore and handicraft events.
18-22 May The city anniversary.
13 Jun Santo Antônio.
24 Jun São João, a particularly huge *forró* festival, part of Caruaru's **Festas Juninas**. The whole town lights up with dancing, traditional foods, parties like the **Sapadrilha**, when the women dress as men, and the **Gaydrilha**, where the men dress as women, and there is even a *Trem do Forró*, which runs from Recife to Caruaru, rocking the whole way to the rhythms.
Sep Micaru, a street carnival. Also in Sep is **Vaquejada**, a Brazilian cross between rodeo and bullfighting; biggest in the northeast.

Recife *p20, maps p21 and p23*
Markets
The permanent craft market is in the **Casa da Cultura**; prices for ceramic figurines are lower than Caruaru.
Cais de Alfândega, Recife Barrio. With local artisans work, 1st weekend of the month.
Domingo na Rua, Sun market in Recife Barrio, stalls of local *artesanato* and performances.
Hippy fair, Praça Boa Viagem, seafront. Sat-Sun only. Life-sized wooden statues of saints.
Mercado São José (1875), for local products and handicrafts.
Sítio Trindade, Casa Amarela. Sat craft fair

Carnaval in Pernambuco

The most traditional and least touristy big carnival in Brazil takes place in Recife, its twin city Olinda, and the little towns nearby. Whilst there are few international tourists, Brazilian visitor numbers are as high as those in Bahia. The music is the most exciting in Brazil, and it is Pernambuco's own. Whilst Salvador pounds to *afoxé* and *axé*, and Rio to samba, Recife and Olinda reverberate to pounding *maracatú*, up-tempo, brassy *frevo* and alternative raucous *mangue beat*. The dancing is some of the best and most acrobatic in the country, with *frevo* dancers leaping, falling into the splits, twirling and throwing tiny, sparkly miniature umbrellas.

Pernambuco carnival is held in the street – unlike Rio and like Salvador. The difference is that, whilst you have to pay in Salvadoro, in Pernambuco, the celebrations here are almost all free. The crowds are big but only oppressive at the opening parade. Recife's carnival takes place in the old city centre, which is dotted with gorgeous Portuguese baroque churches and crumbling mansions, while sitting on two islands between the Beberibe and Capibare and the Atlantic. On the Friday, in the streets around the **Pátio de São Pedro** (Marco Zero) in Recife Antigo, there are big, spectacular *maracatú* parades with troupes of up to 100 drummers and blocos dressed in colourful costumes and swirling white dresses. This square forms the focus of Recife carnival for the following week, with a big sound stage hosting wonderful live acts. Carnival officially opens with the huge **Galo da Madrugada** (Cock of the Dawn parade), which is said by locals to be the largest street gathering in the world. Despite its name the parade usually begins at around 1000 on Carnival Saturday. Floats with many of the most famous stars – such as **Lenine**, **Alceu Valença** and **Eddie** – pass through the teeming crowds under a baking tropical sun. Try and get a place in one of the shaded bandstands at the side of the street as the heat can be oppressive. These can be booked up to a fortnight in advance at the central post office on Avenida Guararapes in Recife. Carnival shows continue until dawn on stages dotted around old Recife for the next five nights. In neighbouring Olinda the party is on the steep cobbled streets, between pretty 18th-century houses and opulent churches and overlooking the shimmering Atlantic. Troupes of *frevo* dancers wander through the throng playing and dancing with effortless gymnastic dexterity.

There are parties in other areas throughout both cities. These include the parade of the **Virgens do Bairro Novo** (Bairro Novo Virgins) in Olinda, led by outrageously camp drag queens, and the **Noite dos Tambores Silenciosos** (the Night of the Silent Drums), held in a pretty colonial church square in one of the poorest inner-city neighbourhoods. It's one of the most spectacular percussion events in Latin America, with a strongly African, sacred, ritualistic feel.

The most spectacular of the Carnival celebrations near Recife are held at **Nazaré da Mata**, where there are traditional parades and music.

during the feast days of 12-29 Jun, fireworks, music, dancing, local food. On 23 Apr, here and in the Pátio de São Pedro, one can see the *xangô* dance. Herbal remedies, barks and spices at Afogados market.

Shopping malls
Shopping Center Recife, between Boa Viagem and the airport, www.shopping-recife.com.br. One of the largest in the country, with clothes, CDs, bookshops and lots more.
Shopping Tacaruna, Santo Amaro. Buses to/from Olinda pass.

Bezerros p32
The city's main attraction is handicrafts, which are found in the district of **Encruzilhada de São João**; items in leather, clay, papier mâché and much more.

Caruaru p32
Caruaru is most famous for its markets which, combined, are responsible for about 70% of the city's income. The **Feira da Sulanca** is basically a clothes market supplied mostly by local manufacture, but also on sale are jewellery, souvenirs, food, flowers and anything else that can go for a good price. The most important day is Mon. There is also the **Feira Livre** or **do Troca-Troca** (free, or barter market). On the same site, Parque 18 de Maio, is the **Feira do Artesanato**, leather goods, ceramics, hammocks and basketware, all the popular crafts of the region; it is tourist orientated but it is on a grand scale and is open daily 0800-1800.

▲ Activities and tours

Recife p20, maps p21 and p23
Diving
Offshore are some 20 wrecks, including the remains of Portuguese galleons; the fauna is very rich.
Mergulhe Coma, T081-3552 2355, T081-9102 6809 (mob), atlanticdivingasr@hotmail.com. English-speaking instructors for PADI courses.
Seagate, T081-3426 1657, www.seagaterecife. com.br. Daily departures and night dives.

Football
Recife's 3 clubs are Sport, Santa Cruz and Náutico. **Sport** play at Ilha do Retiro, T081-3227 1213, take Torrões bus from the central post office on Av Guararapes. **Santa Cruz** play at Arruda, T081-3441 6811, take Casa Amarela bus from the central post office. **Náutico** play at Aflitos, T081-3423 8900, take Água Fria or Aflitos bus. Local derbies are sometimes full beyond safe capacities. Avoid *arquibancada* tickets for Santa Cruz-Sport games. For games at Arruda, dress down.

Tour operators
Jacaré e Cobra de Água Eco-Group, T081-3447 3452, T081-3968 7360 (mob), www.truenet.com.br. Regular excursions in Pernambuco.
Souto Costa Viagens e Turismo Ltda, R Felix de Brito Melo 666, T081-3465 5000, and Aeroporto de Guararapes (American Express representative).
Student Travel Bureau (STB), R Padre Bernardino Pessoa 266, T081-3465 4522, stbmaster@stb.com.br. ISIC accepted, discounts on international flights but not domestic Brazilian flights.
Trilhas, T081-3222 6864, recommended for ecologically oriented excursions.

Olinda p28, map p29
Tour operators
Viagens Sob O Sol, Prudente de Moraes 424, T/F081-429 3303, T081-971 8102 (mob), English spoken, transport, car hire.
Victor Turismo, Av Santos Domont 20, loja 06, T081-3494 1467. Day and night trips to Recife.
Victor Turismo, **Felitur**, R Getulio Vargas 1411, Bairro Novo, T/F081-439 1477.

Porto de Galinhas p30
Diving
AICA Diving, Nossa Senhora do Ó, T/F081-552 1290 or T081-968 4876 (mob), run by Mida and Miguel. For diving and canoeing

trips, as well as excursions to Santo Aleixo
island.

Porto Point Diving, Praça Principal de Porto
de Galinhas, T081-552 1111. Diving and
canoeing trips, as well as excursions to Santo
Aleixo island.

⊖ Transport

Recife *p20, maps p21 and p23*
Air
Bus No 52 runs to the airport, US$1.40, from
the city and Bus 033 runs between the airport
and Boa Viagem. International flights to
Lisbon and **Milan**. Domestic flights to
Brasília, **Campina Grande**, **Fernando de
Noronha**, **Fortaleza**, **João Pessoa**,
Juazeiro do Norte, **Maceió**, **Natal**, **Paulo
Afonso**, **Petrolina**, **Rio de Janeiro**,
Salvador and **São Paulo**.

Airline offices Avianca, www.Avianca.
com.br. **Azul**, airport, www.voeazul.com.br.
Gol, T081-3464 4793, www.voegol.com.br
and the airport. **TAM**, T081-342 5011, at
airport, T081-3462 4466. **TAP/Air Portugal**,
Av Conselheiro de Aguiar 1472, Boa Viagem
T081-3465 8800, at airport T081-3341 0654.
TRIP, T081-3464 4610 (for flights to Noronha)
www.voetrip.com.br and the airport.

Bus
To get to the *rodoviária*, take the metrô from
the central railway station, entrance through
Museu do Trem, opposite the Casa da
Cultura, 2 lines leave the city, take train
marked 'Rodoviária', 30 mins. From Boa
Viagem a taxi all the way costs US$20, or go
to central metrô station and change there.
Bus from the centre (1 hr) or from Boa
Viagem. Bus tickets are sold at Cais de Santa
Rita (opposite EMTU).

Bus PE-15 runs between Av Segismundo
Gonçalves in Olinda and Av Dom Ferreira in
Boa Viagem every 15-20 mins.

Buses to the nearby destinations of
Igarassu (every 15 mins) and **Itamaracá**
(every 30 mins) leave from Av Martins de

Barros, in front of Grande Hotel. To **Olinda**
take any bus marked 'Rio Doce', No 981,
which has a circular route around the city
and beaches, or No 33 from Av Nossa
Senhora do Carmo, US$1, or 'Jardim
Atlântico' from the central post office at
Siqueira Campos.

To **Cabo** (every 20 mins) and beaches
south of Recife from Cais de Santa Rita. To
Salvador, daily 1930, 12 hrs, US$18-25, 4 a
day (all at night) (1 *leito*, 70). To **Fortaleza**,
12 hrs, US$20 *convencional*, US$30 *executivo*.
To **Natal**, 4 hrs, US$9. To **Rio**, daily 2100,
44 hrs, US$58-65. To **São Paulo**, daily 1630,
50 hrs, US$60-70. To **Santos**, daily 1430,
52 hrs, US$60. To **Foz do Iguaçu**, Fri and
Sun 1030, 55 hrs, US$90. To **Curitiba**, Fri
and Sun, 52 hrs, US$76. To **Brasília**, daily
2130, 39 hrs, US$49-60. To **Belo Horizonte**,
daily 2115, 34 hrs, US$41. To **São Luís**, 28
hrs, **Progresso** at 1430 and 1945, US$75. To
Belém, 34 hrs (Boa Esperança bus
recommended). To **João Pessoa**, every
30 mins, US$2.50. To **Caruaru**, every hr,
3 hrs, US$3. To **Maceió**, US$9, 3½ hrs
(express), 6 hrs (slow), either by the main
road or by the coast road daily via 'Litoral'.

Car hire
Budget, T081-3341 2505. 24 hrs, just outside
Guararapes airport. Hertz, T081-462 3552.
Localiza, Av Visconde de Jequitinhonha 1145,
T081-3341 0287, and at Guararapes airport,
T081-3341 2082, freephone, T0800-992000.

Olinda *p28, map p29*
Bus To **Recife**, the No 981 bus has a circular
route around the city and beaches. The No 33
runs to Av Nossa Senhora do Carmo, US$1. Or
take the metrô from Praça do Carmo to
Central station.

Taxi To **Boa Viagem** US$8, US$12 at night.
Make sure the meter is set to rate 1, except on
Sun, holidays or after 2100, when rate 2
applies.

Igarassu *p31*

Bus Buses run to Cais de Santa Rita, **Recife**, 45 mins, US$1.

Itamaracá *p31*

Bus Buses run to **Recife** (Av Martins de Barros opposite the Grande Hotel), US$1.10, very crowded) and **Igarassu**.

Caruaru *p32*

Bus Buses from the centre, at the same place the Recife buses stop, to *rodoviária*, US$0.40. Many buses run to **TIP** in **Recife**, 2 hrs express, US$3. Bus to **Maceió**, 0700, 5 hrs, US$9. Bus to **Fazenda Nova** 1030, 1 hr, US$2, returns to Caruaru 1330.

⊙ Directory

Recife *p20, maps p21 and p23*
Banks Open 1000-1600, hours for exchange vary between 1000 and 1400, sometimes later. **Banco do Brasil**, R Barão da Souza Leão 440, Boa Viagem; Av Dantas Barreto, 541, Santo Antonio, exchange and credit/debit cards, TCs. **Bradesco**, Av Cons Aguiar 3236, Boa Viagem, T081-3465 3033; Av Conde de Boa Vista, Boa Vista; R da Concordia 148, Santo Antônio, 24-hr VISA ATMs, but no exchange. **Citibank**, Av Marquês de Olinda 126, T081-3216 1144, takes MasterCard. Av Cons Aguiar, 2024, ATM. Lloyds Bank, R AL Monte 96/1002. MasterCard, Av Conselheiro Aguiar 3924, Boa Viagem, cash against card. There are money changers at **Anacor**, Shopping Center Recife, loja 52, also at Shopping Tacaruna, loja 173. **Monaco**, Praça Joaquim Nabuco, *câmbio*, TCs and cash, all major currencies, no commission but poor rates. **Norte Cambio Turismo**, Av Boa Viagem 5000, also at Shopping Guararapes, Av Barreto de Menezes. **Cultural centres** British Council, Av Domingos Ferreira 4150, Boa Viagem, T081- 3465 7744, www.britcoun. org/br. 0800-1500, reading room with current British newspapers, very helpful. Alliance Française, R Amaro Bezerra 466, Derby, T081-3222 0918. **Embassies and consulates** Denmark, Av Marques de Olinda 85, Edif Alberto Fonseca 2nd floor, T081-3224 0311 (0800-1200, 1400-1800). France, Av Conselheiro Aguiar 2333, 6th floor, T081-3465 3290. Germany, Av Dantas Barreto 191, Edif Santo Antônio, 4th floor, T081-3425 3288. Japan, R Pe Carapuceiro, 733, 14th floor, T081-3327 7264. Netherlands, Av Conselheiro Aguiar 1313/3, Boa Viagem, T081-3326 8096. Spain, R Sirinhaem, 105, 2nd floor, T081-3465 0607. Switzerland, Av Conselheiro Aguiar 4880, loja 32, Boa Viagem, T081-3326 3144. UK, Av Eng Domingos Ferreira 4150, Boa Viagem, T081-3465 7744 (0800-1130). USA, R Gonçalves Maia 163, Boa Vista, T081-3421 2441. **Medical services** Dengue fever has been resurgent in Recife. Previous sufferers should have good insurance as a 2nd infection can lead to the haemorrhagic form, requiring hospitalization. **Hospital Santa Joana**, R Joaquim Nabuco 200, Graças, T081-3421 3666. **Unicordis**, Av Conselheiro Aguiar 1980, Boa Viagem, T081-3326 5237 and Av Conselheiro Rosa de Silva 258, Aflitos, T081-3421 1000, equipped for cardiac emergencies.

Sergipe and Alagoas

Few tourists stop off in these two tiny states between Bahia and Pernambuco, but herein lies their charm. Both have fine beaches, easily accessible from the state capitals: Aracaju and Maceió. And both have a series of very pretty Portuguese towns where visitors are still a novelty. The most impressive are Penedo (on the banks of Brazil's 'other' great river, the São Francisco, which forms the border between the two states), Marechal Deodoro (the birthplace of the founder of the Brazilian Republic) and the Portuguese capital of Sergipe, São Cristóvão (which is Brazil's fourth oldest town and its newest World Heritage Site). Of the capitals, Maceió is by far the more salubrious, with some excellent beaches and lively nightlife. *» For listings, see pages 52-58.*

Aracaju → *For listings, see pages 52-58. Phone code: 079. Population: 462,600.*

Founded in 1855, this state capital stands on the south bank of the Rio Sergipe, about 10 km from its mouth and 327 km north of Salvador. The river itself is pleasant enough and lined with handsome buildings, but the city centre is tawdry and unpleasant, especially at night, and there is very little to see. Most visitors stay at **Praia Atalaia** (see below), a 10-minute taxi (US$15) or 20-minute bus ride south of town.

Overlooked by most international visitors, Aracaju has a lively off-season carnival immediately prior to the one in Salvador, with the same music and floats. The commercial area is on Rua Itabaianinha and Rua João Pessoa, leading up to Rua Divina Pastora and Praça General Valadão.

Ins and outs

Getting there Santa Maria airport ① *12 km from the centre, Av Senador Júlio César Leite, Atalaia, T079-3243 1388,* receives flights from Maceió, Rio de Janeiro, São Paulo, Recife, Salvador, and other towns. Interstate buses arrive at the **rodoviária** ① *4 km west of the centre,* which is linked to the local bus system from the adjacent terminal (buy a ticket before going on to the platform). Bus 004 'T Rod/L Batista' goes to the centre, US$0.50. Buses from Laranjeiras and São Cristóvão (45 minutes) arrive at the **old bus station** at Praça João XXIII. Look for routes written on the side of buses and at bus stations in town. *» See Transport, page 57.*

Tourist information The principal tourist office, **Bureau de Informaçães Turísticas de Sergipe** ① *Centro de Turismo, Praça Olímpio Campos s/n, Centro T079-3179 1947, daily 0800- 2000,* has town maps and staff speak some English. **Emsetur** ① *Trav Baltazar Goís 86, Edif Estado de Sergipe, 11th-13th floors, T079-3179 7553, www.emsetur.se.gov.br, Mon-Fri*

0700-1300, also has information. There is a tourist booth on the seafront on **Praia Atalaia** ① *Arcos da Orla de Atalaia 243, between R Maynard and Rotary, daily 1000-2100, www.visitearacaju.com.br*, but staff do not speak English and information is limited. There are other branches at the airport (0600-2400) and the *rodoviária* (0800-2230).

Private tour operators offer trips around the city, including rafting on the Rio São Francisco and the river delta. The best is **Brisamar Tur** ① *on the beach, Av Rotary s/n, Hotel Beira Mar, Praia de Atalaia, T079-3223 1781, www.brisamartur.com.br*, English spoken.

Aracaju beaches
Praia Atalaia is the nearest beach to Aracju and a much better place to stay. Although it can't compete with Bahia or Alagoas, there is a long beach of fine white sand, lined with *forró* clubs, restaurants and bars. The beach is lively with families and smooching couples who wander along the esplanade at sunset and the entire area feels as safe and old fashioned as a British Butlins seaside resort. There's even an artificial lake in a tiny theme park where you can hire pedal boats.

Continuing south along the Rodovia Presidente José Sarney, is a long stretch of sand between the mouths of the Rio Sergipe and Rio Vaza Barris; the further you go from the Sergipe, the clearer the water. One of the best beaches is the 30-km-long **Nova Atalaia**, on Ilha de Santa Luzia across the river. It is is easily reached by ferry from the **Terminal Hidroviária** ① *Av Rio Branco, near Praça General Valadão*. Boats cross the river to **Barra dos Coqueiros** every 15 minutes (US$1). Services are more frequent at weekends, when it is very lively with with fishing and pleasure craft.

Excursions from Aracaju
By far the most interesting excursion is to the canyons and beaches of the **Rio São Francisco**. The blue waters course their way through the hills of Minas Gerais and the desert backlands of Bahia before cutting through a series of dramatic gorges near the **Xingó** dam, and subsequently through fields of windswept dunes before washing out into the deep green Atlantic in northern Sergipe. **Brisamar Tur** (see above) runs day-trips down the river stopping at deserted beaches along the way; US$30-50 per person, depending on numbers.

About 23 km northwest from Aracaju is **Laranjeiras**, a tiny and sleepy colonial town with a ruined church on a hill. It is reached by taking the São Pedro bus from the old *rodoviária* in the centre of Aracaju (45 minutes). The town was originally founded in 1605 and has several churches dating back to the imperial period, when it was an important producer of sugar. The 19th-century **Capela de Sant'Aninha** has a wooden altar inlaid with gold.

South of Aracaju → *For listings, see pages 52-58.*

São Cristóvão
The old Sergipe capital lies 17 km southwest of Aracaju on the road to Salvador, sitting pretty on a little hill and on the shores of a briny lake. Founded by Cristóvão de Barros in 1590, it is Brazil's fourth oldest town, and one of many pretty, crumbling towns that dot this part of the country. The colonial centre focuses on Praça São Francisco, which was inscribed on the World Heritage List in August 2010. It is surrounded on all sides by unspoilt Portuguese buildings. The **Igreja e Convento de São Francisco** ① *Praça São*

Francisco, *Tue-Fri 0900-1700, Sat and Sun 1300-1700, US$2*, has a beautiful, simple, baroque façade with a scrolled pediment, and an interior covered with lavish paintings. It also houses a sacred art museum, the **Museu de Arte Sacra e Histórico de Sergipe**, which has more than 500 priceless 18th- and 19th-century ecclesiastical objects. Other buildings on the square include the **Museu de Sergipe** (same opening hours), in the stately former **Palácio do Governo**, and the churches of **Misericórdia** (1627) and the **Orfanato Imaculada Conceição** (1646, permission to visit required from the sisters).

The streets surrounding Praça São Francisco are equally unspoilt, with whitewashed mansions, townhouses and churches offset by the oil-paint yellows and blues, green slat-shutters and woodwork. As tourirsts are few and far between, São Cristóvão is far more tranquil than the colonial cities of Minas or Bahia. There are other squares in town. The Praça Senhor dos Passos is lined by more Portuguese buildings and churches, including **Igreja Senhor dos Passos** and **Terceira Ordem do Carmo** (both built 1739), while on the Praça Getúlio Vargas (formerly Praça Matriz) is the 17th-century **Igreja Matriz Nossa Senhora da Vitória** ① *all are open Tue-Fri 0900-1700, Sat and Sun 1500-1700*. Also worth seeing is the old **Assembléia Legislativa** ① *R Coronel Erundino Prado*. The town is lively only during both the Sergipe pre-Carnaval celebrations, Carnaval itself and Easter, when the streets are strewn with mosaics created with hundreds of thousands of flower petals.

Ins and outs São Cristóvão lies 23 km south of Aracaju. Several buses an hour run between Aracaju's *rodoviária* and São Cristóvão (30 minutes, US$2). Agencies in Atalaia organize excursions to São Cristóvão.

Estância → *Phone code: 079. Population: 57,000.*
Estância is 247 km north of Salvador, on the BR-101, almost midway between the Sergipe-Bahia border and Aracaju. It is one of the oldest towns in Brazil. Its colonial buildings are decorated with Portuguese tiles (none are open to the public). The town's heyday was at the turn of the 20th century and it was one of the earliest places in Brazil to get electricity and a telephone system. Estância is also called 'Cidade Jardim' because of its parks. The month-long festival of **São João** in June is a major event.

Maceió → *For listings, see pages 52-58. Phone code: 082. Population: 780,000.*

The capital of Alagoas is one of coastal Brazil's most attractive and safest cities, with a string of beautiful white-sand beaches, a pretty little colonial centre and a low-key feel. There are a handful of low-key beach resorts a short bus ride away; the best is at **Praia do Frances**, near the old Portuguese capital of Marechal Deodoro. The city has a lively street carnival and traditional **Festas Juninas**.

Ins and outs
Getting there Flights arrive at **Zumbi dos Palmares airport** ① *Rodovia BR-104, Km 91, T082-3214 4000, 25 km from the city centre and beaches*, from Aracaju, Brasília, Rio de Janeiro, Florianópolis, Salvador, São Paulo, Recife, Belo Horizonte and Porto Alegre. A bus runs from the airport to most popular city beach, Ponta Verde/Pajuçara, every 30 minutes 0630-2100 (allow 45 minutes); look for name of the beach on the front of the bus. Taxis charge a flat rate

of around US$23. Interstate buses arrive at the **rodoviária** ⓘ *5 km from the centre*, situated on a hill, with good views. Luggage store is available. Take bus Nos 711 or 715 to Ponta Verde/Pajuçara or buses marked 'Ouro Preto p/centro'; these run every few minutes. A taxi from the bus station to Pajuçara costs around US$15. ▶▶ *See Transport, page 57.*

Getting around and orientation Ponta Verde, Pajuçara and adjacent Praia de Jaticúa are easy to walk around as is the commercial centre. You will need to take public transport between them. Local buses connect Ponta Verde and Pajuçara with the tiny historic city centre every few minutes, leaving from the the the beachside road Avenida Robert Kennedy/ Alvaro Otacilio and stopping at various points including the cathedral. Bus stops are little blue elongated concrete stands. *Combis* for the nearby beaches like Praia do Frances and Marechal Deodoro leave from in front of the Hospital Santa Casa.

Tourist information Semptur ⓘ *Av da Paz 1422, Centro, T082-3336 4409, www.maceio turismo.com.br*, offers information on the city and environs, including maps. The state tourism authority **Setur** ⓘ *R Boa Vista 453, Centro, T082-3315 5700, www.turismo. al.gov.br,* also has branches at the airport and *rodoviária*. The website has a comprehensive list of public services, hotels, restaurants, bars and other contacts. Far more convenient is the **tourist information post** on Pajuçara beach, next to the Sete Coqueiros artisan centre. For very entertaining city tours or trips to Marechal Deodoro, Praia do Francês and beyond contact **Del** (see Activities and tours, page 57), who speaks several languages including English.

Maceió beaches

The sea in Maceió is an impossibly brilliant shade of misty greens and blues and it washes onto some of the finest white-sand beaches in urban Brazil. **Trapiche**, **Sobral** and **Avenida**, immediately in front of the city, look appetizing and are pounded by an impressive surf but they are far too filthy for anything but brown trout. The best beaches for bathing (and the best places to stay in Maceió) are **Pajuçara**, **Ponta Verde** and **Jatiúca**, becoming increasingly plush the further they are from the centre.

Pajuçara has the bulk of the budget accommodation and a nightly crafts market. At weekends there are wandering musicians and entertainers here, and patrols by the cavalry on magnificent *Manga Larga Marchador* horses. Periodically, especially on *candomblé* anniversaries, there are rituals to the *orixá* of the sea, *Yemanjá*. There is a natural swimming pool 2 km off the beach, **Piscina Natural de Pajuçara**, and low tide leaves lots of natural pools to explore in the exposed reef. Check the tides; there is no point going at high tide. *Jangadas* (simple platforms with sails) cost US$10 per person per day (or about US$40 to have a *jangada* to yourself). On Sunday or local holidays in the high season it is overcrowded. At weekends lots of *jangadas* anchor at the reef, selling food and drink.

The next beach is **Ponta Verde**, which is quieter and forms the cape separating Pajuçara from the best of the urban beaches, **Jatiúca**. The better hotels are here and the beach is fronted by a pretty esplanade, lined with cafés and smart restaurants. It is tastefully lit at night. The principal restaurant area in Maceió lies just inland of northern Jatiúca.

After Jatiúca the beaches are: **Cruz das Almas**, **Jacarecica** (9 km from the centre), **Guaxuma** (12 km), **Garça Torta** (14 km), **Riacho Doce** (16 km), **Pratagi** (17 km) and **Ipioca** (23 km). Cruz das Almas and Jacarecica have good surf. Bathing is best three days before and after a full or new moon because tides are higher and the water is more spectacular.

Sights

The centre of Maceió can easily be wandered around in less than an hour. It is pretty, with a handful of handsome Portuguese buildings and some half-decent art deco. On Praça dos Martírios (Floriano Peixoto is the **Palácio do Governo**, which also houses the **Fundação Pierre Chalita** (Alagoan painting and religious art) and the church of **Bom Jesus dos Mártires** (built 1870 and covered in handsome *azulejo* tiles). These are two of the oldest buildings in the city and well worth visiting. The **cathedral**, Nossa Senhora dos Prazeres (1840) is on Praça Dom Pedro II. The **Instituto Histórico e Geográfico** ① *R João Pessoa 382, T082-3223 7797*, has a small but good collection of indigenous and Afro-Brazilian artefacts.

Lagoa do Mundaú, a lagoon, whose entrance is 2 km south at **Pontal da Barra**, limits the city to the south and west. Excellent shrimp and fish are sold at its small restaurants and handicraft stalls and it's a pleasant place for a drink at sundown. Boats make excursions in the lagoon's channels (T082-3231 7334).

Maceió

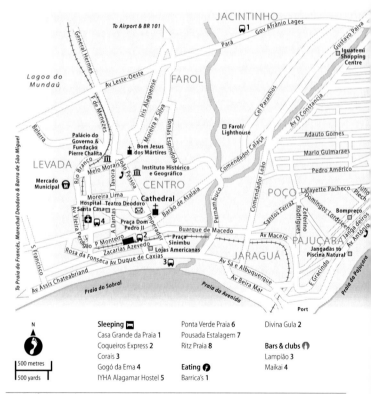

Sleeping	
Casa Grande da Praia	1
Coqueiros Express	2
Corais	3
Gogó da Ema	4
IYHA Alagamar Hostel	5
Ponta Verde Praia	6
Pousada Estalagem	7
Ritz Praia	8

Eating
Barrica's 1
Divina Gula 2

Bars & clubs
Lampião 3
Maikai 4

Excursions from Maceió → For listings, see pages 52-58.

Marechal Deodoro and around

The former capital of Alagoas is 22 km south of Maceió across the impressive brackish lakes that give the state its name, and just behind one of the best resort beaches in the northeast, **Praia do Francês**. The town is well worth a visit, not only for its delightful crumbling buildings and expansive lake, but because of it has a wonderful, laid-back feel and is unspoilt by tourism. It's built on a hill, overlooking **Lake Manguaba**. Boat trips can be organized through tour guides such as **Del** (see Activities and tours, page 57).

The town is named after Marechal Deodoro da Fonseca, the charismatic general who founded the Brazilian republic after the deposition of Emperor Dom Pedro II. The modest townhouse where he grew up is now the **Museu Marechal Deodoro** ① *R Marechal Deodoro, daily 0800-1700, free*. It offers an interesting insight into the simplicity of life in Brazil at the end of the 19th century, even for those in the upper middle classes. Marechal Deodoro's large family lived in a few simple rooms; it is easy to imagine them dining together by oil lamp around the plain hard-wood table, watched over by the family patriarch. Typical northeastern *macramé* lace can be bought outside the museum in the adjacent houses.

The town is very pleasant to wander around, which takes all of 20 minutes. The cobbled streets are lined with attractive colonial houses, some of which have been converted into modest restaurants and *pousadas*. These lead to a series of squares watched over by impressive if decrepit Portuguese churches. Some are almost beyond repair, but the most impressive, the **Igreja Matriz de Nossa Senhora da Conceição** built in 1783 has undergone full restoration, returning to its full baroque glory in late 2008. Be sure to have a peek inside. The 17th-century **Convento de São Francisco** on Praça João XXIII, has another fine baroque church, **Santa Maria Magdalena**, with a superb wooden altarpiece tha t has been badly damaged by termites. You can climb the church tower for views of the town. Adjoining it is the **Museu de Arte Sacra** ① *Mon-Fri, 0900-1300, US$0.50, guided tours available, payment at your discretion*.

It is easy to visit Marechal on a day trip

To Cruz das Almas, Jacarecica, Riacho Doce & Ipioca

To ④ ❷ & Northern Beaches

Av Alvaro Calheiros

❸

Praia de Jatiúca

JATIÚCA
Av Dr A Gomes de Barros

Lourenço Monteiro da Silva

Av Alvaro Otacílio

Av Dr J Marques Luz

H Tradines

Sgto Alberto

José Lages

❺

Praia de Ponta Verde

Sandoval Arroxelas
Vital Barbosa

PONTA
VERDE

J Sampaio Luz

Tenório

Omena

❻

Vasconcelos

Mário de Gusmão ❶

Alagoas

❼

Gouveia

❶

Av Robert Kennedy

❸
❷

❹ ❽

Praia de Ponta Verde

Ⓜ Handicraft

Buses 🚌
Rodoviária **1**
To Marechal Deodoro
  & Praia do Francês **2**
To Riacho Doce **3**
To Praia Francês **4**

from Maceió and still have time left over to enjoy the sun and surf on **Praia do Francês**. It is one of the state's most beautiful beaches, pounded by glass-green surf at one end, protected by a fringing reef at the other and shaded by towering coconut palms along its entire length. There are plenty of *barracas*, restaurants and bars selling drinks and seafood.

There are more beaches beyond Francês, including **Barra de São Miguel**, entirely protected by the reef. It gets crowded at weekends. Several good, cheap *barracas* serve food and drink and there are some decent places to stay. Carnaval is very lively here.

Ins and outs

Minivans run to Marechal Deodoro and Praia do Francês from in front of Hospital Santa Casa next to the Texaco station on Avenida Rio Branco in the city centre. They run 0430-2200 and leave when full (every 20 minutes or so) in high season and at weekends. The journey takes 20 minutes and costs around US$1. Taxis cost around US$30. Tour operators in Maceió offer day trips and can organize air-conditioned private transport (see page 57).

Praia do Francês and Marechal Deodoro have accommodation. For more information see www.praiadofrances.net and www.turismo.al.gov.br.

Penedo → *For listings, see pages 52-58. Phone code: 082. Population: 57,000.*

A more interesting crossing into Alagoas than the usual arrival, along the coast from north or south, can be made by frequent ferry crossings from **Neópolis** in Sergipe, to Penedo some 35 km from the mouth of the Rio São Francisco.

Penedo is a delight – a kind of forgotten Ouro Preto sweltering in the tropical heat on the banks of the sluggish Rio São Francisco, just across the water from Sergipe. Its colonial streets clamber up a series of hills from the banks of the river and are lined with wonderful old buildings. There's a stunning baroque church at every other turn, and barely a tourist in sight. The town was founded in 1565; it was overthrown by the Dutch (who built a fort here) in 1637, and then re-taken by the Portuguese shortly after. It developed as a trading port in the 17th and 18th centuries and grew rich from the gold and diamonds transported down the Rio São Francisco from the interior of Bahia and Minas. Very few of the long two-masted sailing vessels that used to cruise on the river can be seen now, although there are plenty of smaller craft. Boats travel down the river to a series of beautiful white-sand beaches in both Sergipe and Alagoas; these include **Arambipe** and **Peba**. The latter (in Alagoas) is also reachable by road. Either side of the river mouth are turtle nesting grounds, which are protected.

Ins and outs

The *rodoviária* is on the river front on Avenida Beira Rio, near the service station. There is one daily bus from Salvador (via Aracaju). Four buses a day run from Maceió, as well as *combis* 0500-1620. ▶ *See Transport, page 58.*

The very friendly and helpful **tourist office** ① *T082-3551 3907, Praça Barão de Penedo 2, www.penedo.al.gov.br, Mon-Fri 0730-1330*, has useful maps of the city marked with all the principal sights, hotels and restaurants and can organize guided tours of the baroque buildings, sometimes in English.

Sights

The most impressive building in the city is the church of **Nossa Senhora da Corrente** ① *Praça 12 de Abril s/n, Centro, Tue-Sun 0800-1700* (1784), named 'Our Lady of the Current' presumably in homage to the river, which ran swiftly and powerfully past the town until the construction of the Rio São Francisco dam in the late 20th century. It is one of the finest pieces of Portuguese baroque in northeastern Brazil, built on an intimate scale such as those in Ouro Preto, rather than being grand like the churches of Olinda or Salvador. The simple façade hides a rich interior covered in gold leaf and centred on a splendid painted and gilt altarpiece replete with blue and rose marble. The nave is lined with masterful *azulejo* panels, and paintings by the Pernambucan Portuguese artist Libório Lázaro Lial, who was also responsible for much of the ecclesiastical decoration in the city. According to legend, fugitive slaves were hidden inside the church by a trap door behind one of the side altars.

On Praça Barão de Penedo is the neoclassical **Igreja Matriz** (closed to visitors) and the 18th-century **Casa da Aposentadoria** (1782). East and a little below this square is the Praça Rui Barbosa, where you'll find the **Convento de São Francisco** (1783) and the church of **Nossa Senhora dos Anjos** ① *Praça Rui Barbosa s/n, Centro, Tue-Fri 0800-1100 and 1400-1700, Sat and Sun 0800-1100*, whose façade is topped with typically Portuguese-baroque filigree flourishes. As you enter the church, the altar on the right depicts God's eyes on the world, surrounded by the three races (indigenous, black and white). The church a fine trompe l'oeil ceiling (1784), also by Libório Lázaro Lial, which recalls Mestre Atahyde's ceiling in the Igreja São Francisco de Assis in Ouro Preto. The convent is still in use.

The church of **Rosário dos Pretos** ① *Praça Marechal Deodoro*, (1775-1816), is open to visitors, as isis **São Gonçalo Garcia** ① *Av Floriano Peixoto, Mon-Fri 0800-1200, 1400-1700*, (1758-1770). The latter has a particularly fine baroque interior. Lively markets are held outside on weekdays. A wander around them feels like a trip back in time to an older Alagoas. Fishermen sell estuary bream straight out of the wheelbarrow, hacked up bits of cow hang unrefrigerated from meat-hooks in the heat next to stalls offering everything from baskets of home-made soap to pocket calculators. Vast sacks of grain, rice, flour and beans sit next to little hand-drawn carts in front of algae-covered walls of 400-year-old buildings and above the flurry and fluster megaphones blare out special offers and political slogans, broken by the occasional peel of a baroque church bell.

On the same street is the pink **Teatro 7 de Setembro** ① *Av Floriano Peixoto 81, Mon-Fri 0800-1200, 1400-1730, Sat morning only*, with a lovely little conch-shaped auditorium dating from 1884. There are river views from the **Rocheira** just behind **Pousada Estylos**. Before the construction of the São Francisco dam, the river used to wash against the stones immediately below the parapet; you can still see the tide mark, some 4 m higher than it is today.

There are two museums. The most interesting is the **Paço Imperial** ① *Praça 12 de Abril 9, Centro, T082-3551 2498, Tue-Sat 1100-1700, Sun 0800-1200*. Emperor Dom Pedro II stayed in this handsome mansion in 1859 and the building has been trading on the glory ever since. It now preserves a wonderful ceiling painting by Francisco Lopes Ruis, as well as furniture and artefacts that once belonged to the Portuguese high society families and church art. There are great views out over the river from the second floor. The **Casa de Penedo** ① *R João Pessoa 126, signs point the way up the hill from Floriano Peixoto, T082-551 2516, Tue-Sun 0800-1200 and 1400-1800*, displays photographs and books on, or by, local figures.

There are many interesting stopping points along the coast between Maceió and Recife. At **Paripueira**, a 40-minute bus ride from the *rodoviária* in Maceió, the beach is busy only during high season; low tide leaves lots of natural swimming pools.

Barra de Santo Antônio

Some 45 km north of Maceió is this busy fishing village, with a palm-fringed beach on a narrow peninsula, a canoe ride away. The beaches nearby are beautiful: to the south, near the village of Santa Luzia, are **Tabuba** and **Sonho Verde**. To the north is **Carro Quebrado**, from where you can take a beach buggy to **Pedra do Cebola**, or further to **Praia do Morro**, just before the mouth of the Rio Camaragibe.

Maragogi

Unlike many of the resorts just to the north (such as Porto de Galinhas), this little beach town has preserved its local character. Outside the high season, when the Maragogi gets crowded, life goes on pretty much as it has done before tourists began to arrive in the 1980s. And yet the beach is glorious: a seemingly infinite stretch of broad, fine sand washed by a turquoise sea. Some 6 km offshore, a fringing reef reveals a series of deep swimming pools at low tide. The current is rich with sergeant majors and wrasse and with the occasional visiting turtle. Trips out there are easy to organize (expect to pay around US$10).

Ins and outs   From Maceió there are two buses a day and frequent *combis* and shared taxis to Maragogi. *Combis* leave from the Maxi service station (Maxi *posto*) at Cruz de Almas on the BR-101 highway in Maraju on the northern outskirts of Maceió city (taxi from the *rodoviária* US$5). There are also two buses daily from Recife; or take a bus to São José da Coroa Grande, and take a *combi* from there.

Beyond Maragogi, a coastal road, unpaved in parts, runs to the Pernambuco border and **São José da Coroa Grande**. The main highway, BR-101, heads inland from Maceió before crossing the state border to Palmares.

Sergipe and Alagoas listings

For Sleeping and Eating price codes and other relevant information, see page 8-11.

● Sleeping

Aracaju *p44*

The city centre is unpleasant and seedy at night and pretty much all the hotels are scruffy and home to more than just humans. Staying here is not recommended. The beach is only 10-20 mins away.
$ Amado, R Laranjeiras 532, T079-3211 9937, www.infonet.com.br/hotelamado. The best of

a poor selection, with a range of a/c and fan-cooled rooms, a decent breakfast and laundry facilities. Try several rooms before deciding.
$ Brasília, R Laranjeiras 580, T079-3214 2964. It's hard to believe that these corridors of gloomy and often windowless rooms with damp, old air offer the second best sleeping option in the city centre … but they do.

Aracaju beaches *p45*

Hotels are invariably blocky affairs but there are plenty of them, along the main thoroughfare,

Av Santos Dumont, next to the beach.

$$$$ Celi Praia, Av Oceânica 500, T079-2107 8000, www.celihotel.com.br. This big beige block looks like a set of offices – which is appropriate as it caters principally to business clientele. Rooms are plain but large, modern and comfortable. All have balconies, internet and there is a gym, 24-hr business centre, pool, sauna and one of the best restaurants on the beach. Good online rates.

$$ Oceânica, Av Santos Dumont 413, Atalaia, T079-3243 5950, www.pousadaoceanica-se.com.br. A lemon yellow block facing the beach with scrupulously clean simple rooms tiled, painted light blue and furnished with little wooden tables and commodes.

$$ San Manuel, R Niceu Dantas 75, Atalaia, T079-3218 5203, www.sanmanuelpraia hotel.com.br. Pleasant, modern, well-appointed rooms decorated in tile and cream walls with Wi-Fi, international TV and business facilities (including conference rooms). The best views have sea views and terraces.

$ Relicário, Av Santos Dumont 622, Atalaia, T079-3243 1584. A mock-Chinese hotel with simple plain a/c and fan-cooled rooms right next to one of the main beach nightlife areas.

Excursions from Aracaju *p45*

$ Pousada Vale dos Outeiros, Av José do Prado Franco 124, Laranjeiras, T079-3281 1027. A handful of a/c and fan-cooled rooms and a restaurant. Look at several – the best are on the upper floors and have views.

São Cristóvão *p45*

There are no hotels, but families rent rooms near the *rodoviária* at the bottom of the hill.

Estância *p46*

There are a number of cheap, very simple hotels around the Praça Barão do Rio Branco.

$$ Jardim, R Joaquim Calazans 202, Estância, T079-3522 1656, www.hoteljardim-se.com.br. A modern home in a what looks like a converted town house. A range of tile

and whitewash a/c rooms and a a huge buffet breakfast.

$ Turismo Estanciano, Praça Barão do Rio Branco 176, T079-3522 1404, www.hotel estanciano.com. Very simple en suites with little more than a bed, fridge and a table.

Maceió *p46, map p48*

There are many hotels on **Pajuçara** mostly along Av Dr Antônio Gouveia and R Jangadeiros Alagoanos but many of the cheapest are not to be trusted with your belongings. The best rooms are on the beaches **Ponta Verde** and **Jatiúca**. It can be hard to find a room during the Dec-Mar holiday season, when prices go up.

$$$$ Ponta Verde Praia, Av Álvaro Otacílio 2933, Ponta Verde, T082-2121 0040, www.hotel pontaverde.com.br. The best option on the beach in an enviable location with easy walking access to the *forró* clubs and restaurants to the north and Praia Pajuçara to the west. The range of a/c rooms are all well-appointed and comfortable and with international TV and Wi-Fi. The best on the upper floors have wonderful sweeping views out over the sea. Generous buffet breakfast.

$$ Coqueiros Express, R Desportista Humberto Guimarães 830, Ponta Verde, T082- 4009 4700, www. coqueirosexpress.com.br. The best rooms in this spruce, well-run hotel are on the upper floors and have partial sea views. All are well appointed (refurbished in 2006) and decorated in tile and light green and hanging with faux-modernist minimalist *jangada* prints. There's a garden-pond sized pool next to reception and breakfast is hearty.

$$ Pousada Estalagem, R Engenheiro Demócrito Sarmento Barroca 70, T082-3327 6088, www.pousadaestalagem.com.br. Flats with little cookers in a quiet back street above a photo shop. Some have space for up to 6 in one room, making this in the **$** category for groups.

$$ Ritz Praia, R Eng Mário de Gusmão 1300 Laranjeiras, Ponta Verde, T082-2121 4600, www.ritzpraia.com.br. This is a hotel of 2 halves. The refurbished rooms on the upper 4 floors are bright and airy and have views. Those yet to be refurbished are rather gloomy but well-maintained have frowsty en suites with marble fittings. The hotel is only a block from the beach and there is a sun deck on the top floor with a pool the size of a small car.

$ Casa Grande da Praia, R Jangadeiros Alagoanas 1528, Pajuçara, T082-3231 3332, www.hotelcasagrandedapraia.com.br Check the rooms here as some have spongy beds and are rather musty. The best by far are on the upper floor annexe overlooking a small garden. Staff are friendly and offer a decent service which includes a good breakfast. Very close to the beach.

$ Corais, R Desportista Humberto Guimarães 80, Pajuçara, T082-3231 9096. Very basic, musty rooms in corridors around a little garden courtyard. All are frayed, fan-cooled and en suites. Perfect if you plan to spend as little time as possible asleep and as much time as possible on the beach, which is only a few hundred metres away.

$ Gogó da Ema, R Laranjeiras 97, T082-3327 0329, www.hotelgogodaema.com.br. Very simple tile and lime green rooms dominated by large double beds with decent mattresses. En suites come with little marble sinks. The hotel lies in a quiet back street a hop from the sand and offers a generous breakfast.

$ HI Alagamar Hostel, R Pref Abdon Arroxelas 327, T082-3231 2246, www.maceio praiaalbergue.com. It can be hard to get a room here; you'll need to book 2 months in advance in high season and about a week in advance in low season. In either case the hostel requires a 50% upfront deposit into their bank account – a bureaucratic ritual in Brazil. The rooms have all been given a much-needed fresh lick of paint, but look at a few before committing – those on the lower floors are musty and all can be uncomfortably hot at night. Dorms are single-sex.

Marechal Deodoro and around *p49*

$$$ Village Barra Hotel, R Sen Arnon de Mello, Barra de São Miguel, T082-3272 1000, www.villagebarrahotel.com.br. A modern, 4-storey, concrete hotel with rooms over-looking a large pool and sundeck, and the beach at Barra de São Miguel. There's a restaurant and staff can organize excursions to Marechal Deodoro and other locations. The hotel lies 10 km south of Praia do Francês and 16 km from Marechal Deodoro (buses from Praia do Francês and Maceió).

$$ Capitães de Areia, R Vermelha 13, Praia do Francês, 100 m from the beach, T082-3260 1477, www.capitaesdeareia.com.br. A terracotta-coloured block with terraces of rooms near the beach, a pool and a restaurant. Good low season discounts.

$$ Pousada Bougainville e Restaurant Chez Patrick, R Sargaço 3, T082-3260 1251, www.praiadofrances. A pretty little *pousada* near the beach with a/c, rooms with TVs, a pool, seafood and a good French and seafood restaurant cooking.

$$ Pousada da Barra, Av Oceanica 249, Praia Sta Irene, Barra de São Miguel, T022-2771 3109, www.pousadadabarra-rj.com.br. Good.

$$ Pousada Le Soleil, R Carapeba 11, Praia do Francês, T082-3260 1240, www.pousadalesoleil.kit.net. An anonymous concrete block of a hotel with balconies close to the beach. Decent breakfast. Wi-Fi.

Penedo *p50*

$$ Pousada Colonial, Praça 12 de Abril 21, 5 mins' walk from the bus station, T082-3551 2355. A converted colonial building with creaky wooden floors and huge rooms – the best with views out over the river. All are fan-cooled but for the suites. Friendly, efficient reception staff.

$$ São Francisco, Av Floriano Peixoto, T082-3551 2273, www.hotelsaofrancisco.tur.br. A big, ugly 1970s block with boxy little balconied rooms all with a/c, TV and fridge. Showing its age far more than the colonial hotels.

$ Imperial, Praça Coronel Peixoto 43, T082-3551 4749. Simple a/c and fan-cooled rooms with a bath, fan and hot water. The best are on the upper floors and have river views. Cheaper for single rooms and doubles with shared bathrooms.

$ Pousada Estylos I, Praça Jácome Calheiros 79, T082-3551 2465; with another branch, **Pousada Estylos II** at R Damaso do Monte 86, T082-3551 2429. A modest modern hotel near the river with a range of a/c and fan-cooled rooms. Open sporadically, but always in high season.

Barra de Santo Antônio p52

This is a tiny place with no visible addresses. Locals will point you to *pousadas* but it is a struggle to get lost.

$ São Geraldo. Very simple but very clean, and with a restaurant.

$ Pousada Buongiorno, T082-2121 7577 (Maceió). 6 modest rooms in a farmhouse, bathrooms but no electricity, many fruit trees.

Maragogi p52

$$ Agua de Fuego, Rodovia AL 101 Norte, T082-3296 1326, www.aguadefuego.com. The best small hotel in Maragogi with a range of spacious tile floor rooms right overlooking the beach. Friendly Argentinian owner, great breakfast and a pool. In a quiet area 15 mins' walk south of town along the beach.

$$ Jangadeiros, Beira Mar s/n, T082-3296 2167, www.pousadadosjangadeiros.com.br. Plain but modern tile-floor and whitewash rooms in a concrete hotel a block from the beach 5 mins north of the town centre. A little pool and good breakfast. Friendly staff.

$ O Tempo e o Vento, Trav Lourenco Wanderley 22, T082-3296 1720. Tiny little rooms right near the beach. The best are closest to the seafront. Those overlooking the town *praça* can be noisy. Cheaper for single.

🍴 Eating

Aracaju p44

♛♛♛ Cantina d'Italia, Av Santos Dumont s/n, T079-3243 3184. The chicest option on the beachfront serving pizza and pasta to the city's middle classes. The best tables are on the upper deck.

♛♛-♛ O Dragão, Av Santos Dumont, Atalaia, T079-3243 0664. Japanese and Chinese food, including a bottomless sushi and sashimi buffet. Served in a large mock-oriental pavilion right on the beach next to the lake.

♛ Cariri, Av Santos Dumont 243, T079-3243 1379, www.cariri-se.com.br. Northeastern cooking including *frango caipira* (chicken cooked in a tomato and onion sauce) and *carne do sol* (beef jerky). Live *forró* music Tue-Sat. One of several similar lively clubs on this part of the beach.

São Cristóvão p45

♛ Senzala do Preto Velho, R Messias Prado 84. Recommended northeastern specialities.

Maceió p46, map p48

The best restaurants, bars and clubs are on and around R Engenheiro Paulo B Nogueira on **Jatiúca** beach. There are many other bars and restaurants in **Pajuçara** and along Av Antônio Gouveia.

For 5 km from the beginning of Pajuçara, through Ponta Verde and Jatiuca in the north, the beaches are lined with *barracas* (thatched bars) with music, snacks and meals until 2400 (later at weekends). Vendors on the beach sell beer and food during the day; clean and safe.

There are many other bars and *barracas* at Ponto da Barra, on the lagoon side of the city and a string of cheap but high-quality stalls next to the **Lampião club** in Jatiúca in front of the **Maceió Atlantic** suites hotel. Local specialities include oysters, *pitu*, a crayfish (now scarce), and *sururu*, a type of cockle. The local ice cream, 'Shups', is recommended.

¶¶¶ Divina Gula, R Engenheiro Paulo B Nogueira 85, T082-3235 1016, www.divina gula.com.br. Closed Mon. The best restaurant in the city, with a lively atmosphere and busy crowd. The large menu includes many overly-cheesed Italian options, pizzas, seafood and northeastern meat dishes. Portions are large enough for 2.

¶¶-¶ Barrica's, Av Álvaro Calheiros 354, Ponta Verde, www.barricaspizzaria.com.br. One of the liveliest of the waterfront bars in Maceió with live music every night, a buzzing crowd and a range of dishes from pasta to grilled or fried meat or fish, the inevitable pizzas and a handful of veggie options.

Bars and clubs

Maceió *p46, map p48*
The bars here are relaxed and varied and there are nightclubs to suit most tastes.
Lampião, Praia de Jatiúca s/n, diagonally opposite the **Maceió Atlantic** suites hotel. A very lively beachside *forró* bar with live bands every night playing live music to an eager crowd. The house band dress up as Lampião himself – in straw hats and with yokely shirts and leather jerkins and they are fronted by a bottle-blonde in a sparkly cap who has everyone up and dancing. Packed on Fri and Sat. Food available.
Maikai, R Engenheiro Paulo B Nogueira quadra 14, T082-3305 4400, www.maikai maceio.com.br. Restaurant and adjacent club with space for thousands and a range of northeastern acts, playing music from *forró* to *axé*. Currently the busiest and most popular club in town.

Entertainment

Maceió *p46, map p48*
Cinema Arte 1 and 2, Pajuçara and Iguatemi shopping centres. **Cinema São Luiz**, R do Comércio, in the centre. All show foreign films dubbed except the cinema in **Shopping Farol**.

Festivals and events

Aracaju *p44*
1 Jan Bom de Jesus dos Navegantes, procession on the river.
1st weekend in Jan Santos Reis (Three Kings/Wise Men).
Feb/Mar Pre-carnival Carnaval.
Jun Festas Juninas.
8 Dec Both Catholic (**Nossa Senhora da Conceição**) and *umbanda* (*Iemanjá*) festivals.

Excursions from Aracaju *p45*
Jan The main festival in Laranjeiras is **São Benedito** in the 1st week of the month.

São Cristóvão *p45*
Mar Senhor dos Passos, held 15 days after Carnaval.
8 Sep Nossa Senhora de Vitória, the patron saint's day.
Oct/Nov Festival de Arte (moveable).

Estância *p46*
Jun The month-long festival of **São João** is a major event.

Maceió *p46, map p48*
27 Aug Nossa Senhora dos Prazeres.
16 Sep Freedom of Alagoas.
8 Dec Nossa Senhora da Conceição.
15 Dec Maceiofest, a great street party with *trios elêctricos*.
24 Dec Christmas Eve.
31 Dec New Year's Eve, half-day.

Shopping

Aracaju *p44*
The *artesanato* is interesting, with pottery figures and lace a speciality. A fair is held in **Praça Tobias Barreto** every Sun afternoon. The **municipal market** is a block north of the *hidroviária* (ferry terminal).

Penedo *p50*
There is a daily market on the streets off **Av**

Floriano Peixoto, with good hammocks. Ceramics are on sale outside **Bompreço** supermarket, on Av Duque de Caxias.

▲ Activities and tours

Maceió *p46, map p48*
José dos Santos Filho (Del), T082-3241-4966, Mb082-8859 3407, jalbino.filho@hotmail.com. Bespoke tourist guide offering trips along the coast and in the city – including visits to Nelson da Rabeca's house in Marechal Deodoro. Very friendly, knowledgeable and with a comfortable a/c car and reasonable command of English.

⊖ Transport

Aracaju *p44*
Air The airport is 12 km from the centre. Flights to **Brasília**, **Maceió**, **Rio de Janeiro**, **Salvador**, **São Paulo** and **Recife**, with Avianca, www.Avianca.com.br, **Azul**, www.voeazul.com.br, **GOL**, www.voegol.com.br and **TAM**, www.tam.com.br.

Bus Buses run from the old bus station at Praça João XXIII to **Laranjeiras** and **São Cristóvão** (45 mins, US$3).

Long-distance buses run from the *rodoviária*, 4 km from the centre. Buses to the *rodoviária* run from Praça João XXIII, the terminal near the *hidroviária* and from Capela at the top of Praça Olímpio Campos. To **Salvador**, 6-7 hrs, at least 11 a day with Bonfim, US$25, executive service at 1245, US$35 (1 hr quicker). To **Maceió**, US$25 with Bonfim. To **Recife** at 2330, US$35, 10 hrs. To **Rio**, US$20, 30 hrs. To **São Paulo**, US$120, 35 hrs **Belo Horizonte** US$85, 20 hrs, **Foz de Iguaçu**, US$200, 22 hrs. To **Estância**, US$5, 1½ hrs. To **Penedo**, 3 hrs, US$7, 2 a day.

São Cristóvão *p45*
Bus São Pedro buses run to the old *rodoviária* in the centre of **Aracaju** (45 mins, US$1.25).

Estância *p46*
Bus Many buses stop at the *rodoviária*, on the main road. To **Salvador** 4 hrs, US$12-14.

Maceió *p46, map p48*
Air Buses marked 'aeorporto' run to the airport from Ponta Verde/Pajuçara, every 30 mins 0630-2100; allow 45 mins. Taxis charge a flat rate of around US$23. There are flights to **Aracaju**, **Brasília**, **Florianópolis**, **Rio de Janeiro**, **Salvador**, **São Paulo**, **Recife**, **Belo Horizonte** and **Porto Alegre** with Azul, www.voeazul.com.br, **GOL**, www.voegol.com.br, **TAM**, www.tam.com.br, and **Webjet Linhas Aéreas**, www.webjet.com.br.
Bus Taxis from town go to all the northern beaches (for example 30 mins to Riacho Doce), but buses run as far as Ipioca. The Jangadeiras bus marked 'Jacarecica-Center, via Praias' runs past all the beaches as far as **Jacarecica**. From there you can change to 'Riacho Doce-Trapiche', 'Ipioca' or 'Mirante' buses for **Riacho Doce** and **Ipioca**. These last 3 can also be caught in the centre on the seafront avenue below the Praça Sinimbu (US$1 to Riacho Doce). To return take any of these options, or take a bus marked 'Shopping Center' and change there for 'Jardim Vaticana' bus, which goes through Pajuçara. *Combis* to **Marechal Deodoro**, **Praia do Francês** and **Barra de São Miguel** leave from opposite the Hospital Santa Casa in front of the Texaco service station. *Combi* US$2 to Marechal Deodoro, 30 mins, calling at Praia do Francês in each direction. Last bus back from Praia do Francês to Maceió at 1800.

Long distance The 'Ponte Verde/Jacintinho' bus runs via Pajuçara from the centre to the *rodoviária*, also take 'Circular' bus (25 mins Pajuçara to *rodoviária*). Bus to **Recife**, 10 a day, 3½ hrs express (more scenic coastal route, 5 hrs), US$15. To **Aracaju**, US$18, 5 hrs (potholed road). To **Salvador**, 10 hrs, 4 a day, US$50 (*rápido* costs more). To **Penedo**, 4 buses a day and *combis* from outside the *rodoviária*.

Car hire Localiza, and others in the airport and through hotels.

Penedo *p50*

Bus Daily bus to **Salvador** via **Aracaju**, 6 hrs, at 0600, US$25, book in advance. Also a bus direct to Aracaju, 3 hrs, US$7. Buses south are more frequent from **Neópolis**, 6 a day 0630-1800, change here for **Aracaju**, 2 hrs, US$7. To **Maceió**, 115 km, 4 buses a day in either direction, US$12, 3-4 hrs and *combis*.

Ferry Frequent launches for foot passengers and bicycles across the river to **Neópolis**, 10 mins, US$0.50, for connections by bus to **Aracaju**. The dock in Penedo is on Av Duque de Caxias, below Bompreço. The ferry makes 3 stops in Neópolis, the 2nd is closest to the *rodoviária* (which is near the **Clube Vila Nova**, opposite the Texaco station). There is also a car ferry (every 30 mins, US$3, take care when driving on and off).

● Directory

Aracaju *p44*

Banks Visa ATMs at shopping centres, **Banco do Brasil**, Praça Gen Valadão and **Bradesco** in the city centre. MasterCard ATMs at Banco 24 hrs, Av Francisco Porto and Av Geraldo Sobral, in the city centre close to the Shell gas station.

Maceió *p46, map p48*

Banks Open 1000-1500. Good rates at **Banespa**. Plenty of branches of **Bradesco** for ATMs. Cash against MasterCard at **Banorte**, R de Comércio, 306, Centro. **Internet** There are myriad internet cafés throughout the city. **Laundry Lave-Sim**, R Jangadas Alagoanas 962, Pajuçara. Washouse, R Jangadas Alagoanas 698, Pajuçara. **Medical services Unimed**, Av Antonio Brandao 395, Farol, T082-221 1177, used to be São Sebastião hospital. **Pediatria 24 horas**, R Durval Guimaraes 519, Ponta Verde, T082-3231 7742/7702. **Dentist**: Pronto Socorro Odontologico de Maceio, Av Pio XV11, Jatiuca, T082-3325 7534. **Post office** R João Pessoa 57, Centro, 0700-2200.

Penedo *p50*

Banks Bradesco, on Av Duque de Caxias, opposite Bompreço supermarket, with Visa ATM. Open 0830-1300. **Restaurant e Bar Lulu**, Praça 12 de Abril, will change cash if conditions suit the owner, fair rates. **Post office** Av Floriano Peixoto, opposite **Hotel Imperial**. **Telephone** On Barão de Penedo.

Maragogi *p52*

Banks Bradesco in the town centre.

Fernando de Noronha

This small volcanic island rising from the deep, on the eastern edge of the mid-Atlantic ridge 350 km off the coast, is the St Barts of Brazil and one of the world's great romantic destinations. It is blessed with exceptional natural beauty; rugged like the west of Ireland, covered in maquis like Corsica and fringed by some of the cleanest and most beautiful beaches in the Atlantic. Many of the beaches are exposed to the full force of the ocean and pummelled by a powerful bottle-green surf that has earned the island the nickname 'the Hawaii of the Atlantic'. Surf championships are held on Cacimba do Padre beach. However, there are numerous coves where the sea is kinder and the broad beaches are dotted with deep clear-water rock pools busy with juvenile reef fish. The water changes through shades of aquamarine to deep indigo and is as limpid as any on earth. Diving here rivals Mexico's Cozumel and the Turks and Caicos.

Despite the fact that two-thirds of the island is settled, it is an important nesting ground for turtles and marine birds: both the island itself and the seas around it are a marine park, protected by Instituto Chico Mendes de Conservação da Biodiversidade (ICMBio). All that is needed to make it a sanctuary of international standing is to remove the non-native feral monitor lizards (brought here in the 20th century to kill rats), the goats and the abundant cats and dogs. Tourism, however, is controlled and only limited numbers can visit the island at any time. Book well in advance. *For listings, see pages 62-62.*

Ins and outs

Getting there and around Flights to the island from Recife and Natal are run by TRIP, www.voetrip.com.br. CVC, www.cruisevacationcenter.com, operates a small cruise liner, which sails from Recife to Noronha and then back to Recife via Fortaleza and Natal. Buggy hire, motorbike hire and jeep tours are available in town.

Best time to visit The rains are April to July. The vegetation turns brown in the dry season (August to March), but the sun shines all year round. Noronha is one hour later than Brazilian Standard Time. There are far fewer mosquitos here than on the coast but bring repellent.

Tourist information Instituto Chico Mendes de Conservação da Biodiversidade (ICMBio) has imposed rigorous rules to prevent damage to the nature reserve and everything, from development to cultivation of food crops to fishing, is strictly administered. Many locals are now dependent on tourism and most food is brought from the mainland. Entry to the island is limited and there is a tax of US$30 per day for the first week of your stay. In the second week the tax increases each day. Take sufficient reais as it's difficult to change money. For information see www.fernandodenoronha.com.br.

Sights

The island was discovered in 1503 by Amerigo Vespucci and was for a time a pirate lair. In 1738 the Portuguese built a charming little baroque church, **Nossa Senhora dos Remedios**, some attractive administrative buildings and a fort, **O Forte dos Remédios**,

Fernando de Noronha

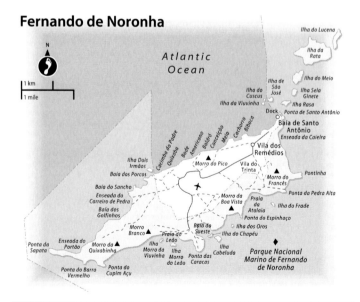

which was used as a prison for political dissidents by the military dictatorship in the late 20th century. The most famous was the communist leader Luis Carlos Prestes, who led the famous long march, the Prestes Column, in 1925-1927. Many people were tortured and murdered here. The islands were occupied by the USA during the Second World War and used as a naval base. US guns sit outside the *prefeitura* in the centre of the main town, **Vila dos Remédios**, which overlooks the coast on the eastern shore.

Some of the best beaches lie immediately south of the town, clustered around an imposing granite pinnacle, the **Morro do Pico**. The most beautiful are **Conceição**, **Boldró**, **Americano**, **Baía do Sancho**, **Cacimba do Padre** and the turquoise cove at **Baía dos Porcos**, which sits on the edge of the beginning of the marine park. Beyond is the **Baía dos Golfinhos**, with a lookout point for watching the spinner dolphins in the bay. On the south, or windward side, there are fewer beaches, higher cliffs and the whole coastline and offshore islands are part of the marine park. As with dive sites, **Instituto Chico Mendes de Conservação da Biodiversidade (ICMBio)** restricts bathing in low-tide pools and other sensitive areas to protect the environment.

There are good possibilities for hiking, horse riding and mountain biking. A guide will take you to the marine park and to beaches such as **Atalaia**, which has the best snorkelling.

Wildlife and conservation

The island is a UNESCO World Heritage Site. It may look like an ecological paradise but it has been the victim of much degradation. Almost all of the native vegetation was chopped down in the 19th century, when the island was used as a prison, to prevent prisoners from hiding or making rafts. A giant native rodent, recorded by Amerigo Vespucci was wiped out and linseed, feral cats, dogs, goats, rats, mice, tegu (*teju* in Portuguese) lizards and cavies were introduced in the 16th century. These continue to damage bird and turtle nesting sites and native vegetation. Nonetheless, the island remains an important sanctuary for sea-bird species. Ruddy turnstone, black and brown noddy, sooty tern, fairy tern, masked booby, brown booby and white-tailed tropicbird all nest here. Some endemic bird species still survive: the Noronha vireo (*Vireo gracilirostris*); a tyrant flycatcher, the Noronha elaenia or cucuruta (*Elaenia spectabilis reidleyana*); and the Noronha eared dove or arribaçã (*Zenaida auriculata noronha*). There is an endemic lizard (*Mabuya maculate*) and at least 5% of the fish species are unique to the archipelago. The most spectacular animals are the nesting hawksbill and green turtles, and the spinner dolphins. Good terrestrial wildlife guides are non-existent on Noronha and even **Instituto Chico Mendes de Conservação da Biodiversidade (ICMBio)** spell the species names incorrectly on their information sheets. There are a number of reasonable dive shops; though biological knowledge is minimal.

Fernando de Noronha listings

For Sleeping and Eating price codes and other relevant information, see pages 8-11.

😴 Sleeping

Fernando de Noronha *p59, map p60*
Some of the most luxurious hotels on the island are built on illegally occupied land and are not listed here.

$$$$ Solar dos Ventos, T081-3619 1347, www.pousadasolardosventos.com.br. With a spectacular bay view, well-appointed wood, brick and tile bungalows and friendly owners.

$$$$ Zé Maria, R Nice Cordeirol, Floresta Velha, T081-3619 1258, www.pousadazemaria. com.br. Spacious bungalows with cream tile floors, hardwood ceilings and generous beds. Verandas and hammocks have views out to the Morro do Pico. The highlight is the delicious, but small deep-blue half-moon pool.

$$$ Pousada dos Corais, Conj Residencial Floresta Nova, T081-3619 1147, www.pousada corais.com.br. 8 simple a/c rooms, small pool.

$$$ Pousada do Vale, T081-3619 1293, www.pousadadovale.com. Friendly, well-run *pousada* with comfortable en suite rooms decorated with mosaics. The best are the duplex wooden bungalows. 300 m from Vila dos Remedios town centre.

🍴 Eating

Fernando de Noronha *p59, map p60*
††† Ecologiku's, Estr Velha do Sueste, T081-3619 1807. Bahian cooking served in an open-sided, mood-lit restaurant with a little garden.

† Açai e Raizes, BR-363, Floresta Velha. Roadside sandwich bar with snacks, puddings and delicious cream of Cupuaçu and Açai.

† Cia da Lua, Bosque dos Flamboyantes. Coffee, snacks, internet, car and buggy rental.

† Jacaré, Praça Presidente Eurico Dutra. The best-value on the island, with seafood buffet.

🍹 Bars and clubs

Fernando de Noronha *p59, map p60*
Vila dos Remédios town, which is the size of a postage stamp, has several bars with lively weekend *forró* from 2200 on weekends, and a bar with live reggae nightly in high season.

⛰ Activities and tours

Fernando de Noronha *p59, map p60*
Tour and dive operators
It is possible to see hatching turtles in season. For details, contact **Fundação Pró-Tamar**, Caixa Postal 50, CEP 53990-000, Fernando de Noronha, T081-3619 1269.

Atlantis Divers, T081-3619 1371, www.atlantis divers.com.br. **Águas Claras** and **Noronha Divers** all offer the same dive locations around Noronha and the offshore islands, as well as dive 'baptism' for complete beginners. Diving costs US$50-75 for 2 tanks and is by far the best in Brazil aside from Atol das Rocas, 2 days off Bahia.

Barco Naonda, Vila do Porto, T081-3619 1307, www.barconaonda.com.br. One of many companies offering boat trips around the island. The best leave at lunchtime, catching the late afternoon light on their return.

Locadora Ilha do Sol, T081-3619 1132, www.pousadadovale.com. Offers buggy rental and guided tours of the island.

🚌 Transport

Fernando de Noronha *p59, map p60*
Air Daily flights to **Recife** with **TRIP** (1 hr 20 mins, US$400 return). To **Natal** with **TRIP** (1 hr, US$300 return).

Paraíba

Travellers used to bypass Paraíba, but they are beginning to discover that there are many reasons to stop. The beaches are some of Brazil's best and least spoilt. Some of the most important archaeological sites in the Americas are tucked away in the haunting, rugged landscapes of its interior and the state capital, João Pessoa, is an attractive colonial city with a lively nightlife. Each year in June, Campina Grande, on the edge of the sertão, hosts one of the country's biggest festivals, the Festa do São João, with live music and up to a million people dancing forró into the small hours.

The dense tropical forest that once covered the entire coastal strip now only survives in patches, one of which is within the city of João Pessoa; forming one of the largest areas of wilderness within any city in the world. The seaboard is marked for much of its length by offshore reefs. Inland from the coastal plain the Zona da Mata is an abrupt line of hills and plateaux, a transitional region between the humid coast and the much drier interior. Most people live in this zone, especially in and around the state capital and a couple of other industrial centres.

▸ For listings, see pages 70-75.

João Pessoa and around → *For listings, see pages 70-75. Phone code: 083. Population: 598,000.*

João Pessoa is the state capital yet retains a small town atmosphere. It has some attractive colonial architecture and is set on the Rio Paraíba amid tropical forest. The atmosphere is restful and laid-back, yet there are plenty of bars and restaurants along the beachfront, particularly popular at weekends. The main beach, **Tambaú**, is pleasant but rather built up.

Ins and outs

Getting there and around It is a two-hour bus ride through sugar plantations on a good road from Recife (126 km) to João Pessoa. **Presidente Castro Pinto airport** ① *11 km south of the centre, T083-3232 1200,* receives flights from São Paulo, Brasília, Recife and Rio de Janeiro. A taxi from the airport to centre costs US$15, to Tambaú US$20. Alternatively, the airlines **GOL** flies from São Paulo or Rio to Recife, then provides free bus transport to João Pessoa. The **rodoviária** ① *R Francisco Londres, Varadouro, 10 mins west of the centre, T083-3221 9611,* has a luggage store and helpful **PBTUR**, www.pbtur.pb.gov.br, information booth. A taxi to the centre costs US$3.50, to Tambaú US$9. All city buses stop at the *rodoviária* and most go via the Lagoa (Parque Solon de Lucena). From the centre, take No 510 for Tambaú, No 507 for Cabo Branco. The **ferroviária** ① *Av Sanhaúá, Varadouro, T083-3221 4257,* has train connections to Bayeux and Santa Rita in the west, and Cabedelo to the north.

Tourist information PBTUR ① *Centro Turístico Almte Tamandaré 100, Tambaú, T083-3214 8279 or T0800-3281 9229, 0800-1900,* and others at the *rodoviária,* and airport, provide useful information, pamphlets and maps. Some staff speak good English, and some French.

② João Pessoa centre

➡ João Pessoa maps
2 João Pessoa centre, page 64
3 Tambaú and Manaíra, page 66

Sleeping 🛏
Guarany 2

JR 3

Not to scale

Background
The Portuguese did not gain a foothold on this part of the coast until the end of the 16th century. Their fort became the city of Filipéia, which grew to become the third largest in Brazil. This was later re-named Parahyba and then João Pessoa, in honour of the once state governor who refused to form alliances with other powerful politicians during the 1930s run for the vice-presidency. This led to his assassination, an event that swept his running mate, the fascist, Getúlio Vargas to power. Pessoa's 'nego' ('I refuse') is written on the state's flag.

Sights
The well-preserved Centro Histórico has several churches and monasteries that are worth seeing. The **Centro Cultural São Francisco** ① *Praça São Francisco 221*, one of the most important baroque structures in Brazil, includes the beautiful 16th-century church of São Francisco and the Convento de Santo Antônio, which houses the **Museu Sacro e de Arte Popular** ① *T083-3218 4505, Tue-Sun 0900-1200 and 1400-1700, U$2*, with a magnificent collection of colonial artefacts. This is the best point to see the sunset over the forest.

Other tourist points include the **Casa da Pólvora**, an old gunpowder store which has become the city museum, and **Museu Fotográfico Walfredo Rodríguez** ① *Ladeira de São Francisco, Mon-Fri 0800-1200 and 1330-1700*. The **Teatro Santa Rosa** ① *Praça Pedro Américo, Varadouro, T083-3218 4382, Mon-Fri 0800-1200 and 1330-1800*, was built in 1886 with a wooden ceiling and walls. The **Espaço Cultural José Lins de Rego** ① *R Abdias Gomes de Almeida 800, Tambauzinho, T083-3211 6222*, a cultural centre named after the novelist, includes an art gallery, history and science museums, several theatres, cinema and a planetarium. The **Fundação José Américo de Almeida** ① *Av Cabo Branco 3336, Cabo Branco*, should be visited by those interested in modern literature and politics; it is in the former house of the novelist and sociologist.

João Pessoa prides itself in being a green city and is called 'Cidade Verde'. Its parks include the 17-ha **Parque Arruda Câmara**, also known as Bica, located north of the centre in the neighbourhood of Roger; it has walking trails, an 18th-century fountain, an aviary and a small zoo. **Parque Solon de Lucena** or **Lagoa** is a lake surrounded by impressive palms in the centre of town, the city's main avenues and bus lines go around it. **Mata** or **Manancial do Bouraquinho** is a 471-ha nature reserve of native *Mata Atlântica*, one of the largest urban forest reserves in Brazil. It is located south of the centre and administered by Instituto Chico Mendes de Conservação da Biodiversidade (ICMBio) ① *T083-3244 2725*, which organizes guided walks; access is otherwise restricted.

Urban beaches
João Pessoa's urban beachfront stretches for some 30 km from Ponta do Seixas (south) to Cabedelo (north); the ocean is turquoise green and there is a backdrop of lush coastal vegetation. By the more populated urban areas the water is polluted, but away from town the beaches are reasonably clean; some spots are calm and suitable for swimming while others are best for surfing. The beach of **Tambaú** lies right in the centre of this 30-km strip and is, for all intents and purposes, the centre of the João Pessoa. It has many hotels, restaurants, the state tourism centre and clean sand. It is about 7 km from the old colonial city centre along Avenida Presidente Epitáceo Pessoa. The pier by **Hotel Tambaú** affords pleasant views (bus No 510 'Tambaú' from outside the *rodoviária* or the city centre, alight at Hotel Tropical Tambaú). South of Tambaú are **Praia de Cabo Branco** and **Praia do Seixas**

③ Tambaú & Manaíra

➡️ João Pessoa maps
2 João Pessoa centre, page 64
3 Tambaú and Manaíra, page 66

200 metres
200 yards

Sleeping 🛏️
Best Western Caiçara **2**
Littoral **1**
Nobile Inn Royal Praia **5**
Pousada Mar Azul **10**
Solar Filipéia **9**
Tambía Praia **7**
Tropical Tambaú **3**
Victory Business Flat **6**
Villa Mare Apt Hotel **8**
Xênius **4**

Eating 🍴
Adega do Alfredo **1**
Cheiro Verde **4**
Gulliver **2**
Mangaí **3**

Bars & clubs 🍸
Fashion Club **5**
Incognito **6**
Mr Caipira **8**
Zodiaco **7**

and, to the north, are the beaches of **Manaíra**, **Bessa**, **Intermares**, **Poço** and **Camboinha**, before reaching the port of Cabedelo (see below).

Excursions from João Pessoa

About 14 km south of the centre, down the coast, is the **Cabo Branco** lighthouse at the little forested cape of **Ponta do Seixas**, the **cape of the rising sun**, the most easterly point of continental Brazil and South America (34° 46' 36" W), and thus the first place in the Americas where the sun rises. There is a panoramic view from the clifftop and the beautiful beach below, **Praia Ponta do Seixas**, and coming here to watch sunrise is one of João Pessoa's most traditional romantic experiences. This beach and adjacent, more urbanized, **Praia do Cabo Branco** to the north and **Praia do Penha** to the south are much better for swimming than Tambaú. Penha has a 19th-century church where devotees petition the saints for succour, leaving notes all over the building and crawling up the steps to the nave in obeisance. Take bus No 507 'Cabo Branco' from outside the *rodoviária* to the end of the line and hike up to the lighthouse from there. Or at low tide you can walk from Tambaú to Ponta do Seixas in about two hours.

The port of **Cabedelo**, on a peninsula between the Rio Paraíba and the Atlantic Ocean, is 18 km north by road or rail. Here, Km 0 marks the beginning of the **Transamazônica highway**. At the tip of the peninsula are the impressive but run-down walls of the 17th-century fortress of **Santa Catarina**, in the middle of the commercial port. The **Mercado de Artesanato** is at Praça Getúlio Vergas in the centre.

The estuary of the Rio Paraíba has several islands; there is a regular boat service between Cabedelo and the fishing villages of **Costinha** and **Forte Velho** on the north bank; Costinha had a whaling station until the early 1980s.

The beaches between João Pessoa and Cabedelo have many bars and restaurants and are very popular with the locals on summer weekends (Bar do Sumé, Rua Beira Mar 171, Praia Ponta do Mato, Cabedelo, has good fish and seafood). Take a bus marked Cabedelo-Poço for the beach as most Cabedelo buses go inland along the Transamazônica. A taxi from Tambaú to Cabedelo costs US$24.

At Km 3 of the Transamazônica, about 12 km from João Pessoa, is the access to **Jacaré**, a pleasant beach on the Rio Paraíba (take the 'Cabedelo' bus and walk 1.5 km or take the train and walk 1 km, taxi from Tambaú US$10). There are several bars along the riverfront where people congregate to watch the lovely sunset to the sounds of Ravel's *Bolero*. Here you can hire a boat along the river to visit the mangroves or ride in an ultralight aircraft. ▶ *See Activities and tours, page 74.*

From Tambaú tour boats leave for **Picãozinho**, a group of coral reefs about 700 m from the coast which at low tide turn into pools of crystalline water, suitable for snorkelling (US$20 per person). Further north, boats leave from Praia de Camboinha to **Areia Vermelha**, a large sandbank surrounded by corals. This becomes exposed at low tide, around the full and new moon, and is a popular bathing spot (US$20 per person tour, US$5 per person transport in a *jangada*). Floating bars are set up at both locations, travel agencies arrange trips.

Paraíba coast → *For listings, see pages 70-75.*

The Paraíba coastline has 117 km of beautiful beaches and coves, surrounded by cliffs and coconut groves. These are among the least developed of the northeast.

Tambaba
The best-known beach of the state is Tambaba, the only official nudist beach of the northeast and one of only two in Brazil. It is located 49 km south of João Pessoa in a lovely setting: the green ocean, warm water, natural pools for swimming formed by the rocks, cliffs up to 20 m high full of caves, palms and lush vegetation. Two coves make up this famous beach: in the first bathing-suits are optional, while the second one is only for nudists. Strict rules of conduct are enforced, unaccompanied men are not allowed in this area and any inappropriate behaviour is reason enough to be asked to leave. The only infrastructure is one bar, where meals are available.

Access is from **Jacumã**, via the BR-101, 20 km south from João Pessoa to where the PB-018 goes 3 km east to Conde and continues 11 km to the beach of Jacumã; from here a dirt road goes 12 km south to Tambaba. Buses run hourly to Jacumã from the João Pessoa *rodoviária*. In summer, dune buggies can be hired at Jacumã to go to Tambaba. Buggy from João Pessoa to Tambaba US$25 per person return (leaves 0930, returns 1730). A day-trip by taxi costs US$95.

Between Jacumã and Tambaba are several good beaches such as **Tabatinga**, which has many summer homes built on the cliffs, and **Coqueirinho**, which is surrounded by pleasant vegetation, and is good for bathing, surfing and exploring caves. There are plenty of cheap and mid-range *pousadas* at both and a very good seafood restaurant at Coqueirinho, **Canyon de Coqueirinho**, on the beach. Near the border with Pernambuco is the 10-km long beach of **Pitimbu**.

Campina and around

The best beaches of northern Paraíba are in the vicinity of the fishing village of **Campina**; although there is little infrastructure in this area, the shore is worth a visit. Access is via a turnoff to the east at Km 73.5 of the BR-101, 42 km north of João Pessoa. It is 28 km along a dirt road (PB-025) to Praia Campina, with a wide beach of fine sand, palms and hills in the background. Nearly 3 km south is **Praia do Oiteiro**, in which the white sand stands out in contrast with the multicoloured cliffs and calm blue ocean. About 2 km north of Campina is **Barra do Mamanguape**, where Instituto Chico Mendes de Conservação da Biodiversidade (ICMBio) runs a preservation centre for marine manatee.

Some 85 km from João Pessoa is **Baia da Traição**, a fishing village and access point for a number of beaches. Its name means 'Bay of Betrayal' and refers to the massacre of 500 residents of a sugar plantation in the 16th century. There is a reserve near town where wood and string crafts are made by the local indigenous people; an annual festival, **Festa do Toré**, takes place on 19 April. Fisherman offer boat tours to the area's less accessible beaches (US$15 per person). **Barra de Camaratuba**, 17 km north of Baia da Traição, is a popular surfing beach.

The sertão → *For listings, see pages 70-75.*

The semi-arid region of thorn and bush that makes up the hinterland of the northeast is known as the *sertão*. The Transamazônica runs right through the heart of the region, due west of João Pessoa as the BR-230, and along the axis of the state of Paraíba.

Campina Grande → *Phone code: 083. Population: 340,500.*

Set in the Serra da Borborema, 551 m above sea level and 130 km west of João Pessoa, the second city in Paraíba has a very pleasant climate. Known as the '*porta do sertão*' (door of the sertão), it is an important centre for light industry and an outlet for goods from most of northeast Brazil. In the 1920s it was one of the most important cotton producing areas in the world; a decline in this industry brought a decrease in prosperity in the 1940s and 1950s and the diversification of industry to areas such as sisal and leather. The city's two universities have been instrumental in technological development and reactivation of the local economy and today Campina Grande has the honour of making every single pair of Brazil's famous fashion flip-flops, Havaianas, which are sold all over the world.

Ins and outs The **João Suassuna airport** ① *7 km south of centre on the road to Caruaru, T083-3331 1149*, receives daily flights from Recife. A taxi from the airport to the centre costs US$15. A city bus runs to Praça Clementino Procópio, behind Cine Capitólio. The **rodoviária** ① *Av Argemiro de Figueiredo, T083-3321 5780*, is a 20-minute bus ride from the centre. Tourist information is available from PBTUR ① *T156*, or DEMTUR ① *T083-3341 3993*.

Sights Avenida Floriano Peixoto is the main street running east–west through the entire city, with Praça da Bandeira at its centre. The **Museu Histórico de Campina Grande** ① *Av Floriano Peixoto 825, Centro, T083-3310 6182, Tue-Sat 0800-1200, 1300-1700*, is the city museum housed in a 19th-century building, with a very well-displayed photo and artefact collection reflecting the cycles of prosperity and poverty in the region. The **Museu da História e Tecnologia do Algodão** ① *R Benjamin Constant s/n, Estação Ferroviária, T083-*

3341 1039, Tue-Sat 0800-1200 and 1300-1700, free, has machines and related equipment used in the cotton industry in the 16th and 17th centuries. The **Museu Regional de São João** ① *Largo da Estação Velha, Centro, T083-3341 2000, daily 0800-1300,* houses an interesting collection of objects and photographs pertaining to the June celebrations.

The **Teatro Municipal Severino Cabral** ① *Av Floriano Peixoto,* is a modern theatre where there are regular performances. The main parks in town are: the **Parque do Açude Novo** (Evaldo Cruz), a green area with playgrounds, fountains and restaurants; the nearby **Parque do Povo** with its *forródromo* where the main festivities of the city take place; and the **Açude Velho**, a park around a dam south of the centre. The **Mercado Central**, where a large roof has been built over several blocks of old buildings, has regional crafts and produce, is worth a visit.

Excursions from Campina Grande

About 10 km north from Campina Grande is **Lagoa Seca**, where figures in wood and sacking are made, and there is a **Museu do Índio**.

Some 35 km east of Campina Grande, off the road to João Pessoa, is **Ingá**, site of the **Pedra de Itacoatiara** archaeological centre, where inscriptions dated as 10,000 years old were found on a boulder 25 m long and 3 m high. A small museum at the site contains fossils of a giant sloth and a Tyrannosaurus rex. During the June festivities there is a train service to Itacoatiara.

The **Boqueirão** dam on the Rio Paraíba, 70 km southeast of town, is where locals flock on holidays for watersports; there is a hotel-*fazenda* (T081-3391 1233).

Cariri

The *sertão* proper begins near São João do Cariri an hour or so from Campina Grande. This is an area of fascinating rock formations, with giant weather-worn boulders sitting on top of gently curved expanses of rock that look out over a plain of low bushes and stunted trees. Although the vegetation is quite different to the landscape itself; the arid conditions and the size of the trees recalls the Australian outback (the rocks themselves have been compared to the Devil's Marbles). The most spectacular of all the formations sit in the private grounds of **Fazenda Pai Mateus** (see Sleeping, page 72). Like various other sites in Paraíba and Rio Grande do Norte, boulders here are covered in important pre-Columbian rock art, some of which has been controversially dated as pre-Clovis (making it older than the accepted datings for the first waves of American population coming from over the Bering Strait). A famous local holy man lived inside one of the giant hollowed-out stones and the views from his former home at sunset are particularly spellbinding. The *fazenda* itself is a very pleasant place to stay and there is rich, though depleted wildlife in the area and good birdwatching. Tours can be organized with **Cariri Ecotours** (see page 89), who provide fascinating information about the archaeological sites but have little knowledge of the fauna in the region. The *fazenda*'s guides are informative about life in the *sertão* and the use of medicinal plants, but again as ever in Brazil, knowledge of birds and animals is poor.

North of Cariri, 46 km from Campina Grande, is **Areial**, the main town of the Brejo Paraibano, a scenic region of green hills and valleys, with a pleasant climate, where colonial sugar *fazendas* have been transformed into hotels.

Patos → *Population: 84,500.*

West of Campina Grande the landscape turns to vast, flat expanses, flanked by rolling hills and interesting rock formations; very scenic when green, but a sad sight during the prolonged *sertão* droughts. Situated 174 km from Campina Grande is Patos, the centre of a cattle-ranching and cotton-growing area. It's also an access point for the **Serra do Teixeira**, 28 km away, which includes **Pico do Jabre**, the highest point in the state, at 1130 m above sea level. There are various hotels and restaurants in Patos.

Souza → *Phone code: 081. Population: 59,000.*

About 130 km northwest of Patos, the pleasant *sertão* town of Souza, has high temperatures year-round and is gaining fame for the nearby dinosaur tracks and prehistoric rock carvings. The *rodoviária* is 1 km from the centre, there are no city buses, walk (hot), take a moto-taxi (US$1) or a taxi (US$5). The **Igreja do Rosário** at the Praça Matriz has paintings dating to the Dutch occupation of the area. It currently functions as a school. About 3 km from the centre, atop a hill, is a **statue of Frei Damião**, an important religious leader of the northeast who died in 1997. Frei Damião was an Italian friar who came to Brazil in the 1930s and stayed to become an inspiration for the faith of its most recent generation of dispossessed. He is seen as belonging to the same tradition as O Conselheiro and Padre Cícero.

Fossilized dinosaur prints of up to 90 different species, which inhabited the area between 110 and 80 million years ago, are found in a number of sites in the Souza region. These were extensively studied by the Italian palaeontologist Giussepe Leonardi in the 1970s and 1980s. The **Vale dos Dinossauros**, on the sedimentary river bed of the Rio do Peixe, is one of the closest sites to Souza; it has some impressive Iguanodontus prints. Access is 4 km from town along the road north to Uiraúna; the best time to visit is the dry season, July to October. The area has no infrastructure and is best visited with a guide. Try to contact Robson Marques of the **Movisaurio Association** ① *R João Rocha 7, Souza, PB 58800-610, T083-3522 1065*, who is very knowledgeable; otherwise contact the Prefeitura Municipal. Tours can be organized through **Cariri Ecotours** in Natal (see page 89), these can be combined with visits to Cariri.

Paraíba listings

For Sleeping and Eating price codes and other relevant information, see pages 8-11.

🛏 Sleeping

João Pessoa *p64, maps p64 and p66*
The town's main attractions are its beaches, where most tourists stay. Hotels in the centre are poorer and tend to cater for business clients. The centre is very quiet after dark and it is difficult to find a restaurant. Cheaper hotels can be found near the *rodoviária*; look carefully as some are sleazy. The most convenient beach and the focus of nightlife

and restaurants is **Tambaú**. There are good restaurants and a few hotels in **Manaíra**, north of Tambaú. There are also a few in the southern beach suburb of **Cabo Branco**, but this is quieter and has fewer eating options.

$$ Guarany, R Almeida Barreto 181 and 13 de Maio, T/F083-2106 8787, www.hotel guarani.com.br. Cheaper in low season, or without a/c and TV. A pleasant, safe, extremely good-value establishment with a self-service restaurant.

$$ Hotel JR, R João Ramalho de Andrade, T083-2106 8700, www.hoteljr.com.br. 1990s business hotel with basic facilities and a restaurant. The largest and most comfortable in the centre.

$ Ouro Preto, R Idaleto 162, T083-3222 7074, Varadouro near *rodoviária*. Very simple rooms with baths and a fan.

Urban beaches *p65, map p66*
Accommodation can also be found in the outer beaches such as **Camboinha** and **Seixas**, and in **Cabedelo**.

$$$ Best Western Caiçara, Av Olinda 235, T/F083-3247 2040, www.hotcaicarara.com.br. A slick, business-orientated red and white apartment block with business facilities, a pleasant restaurant and a rooftop pool with a view.

$$$ Littoral, Av Cabo Branco 2172, T083-2106 1100, www.hotellittoral.com.br. An unprepossessing block in a great seafront location. With a pleasant swimming pool set in leafy gardens and modern, simply appointed rooms with small balconies. There are often discounts for online advanced bookings.

$$$ Nobile Inn Royal Praia, Coração de Jesus, T083-2106 3000, www.royalhotel.com. br. Comfortable a/c rooms with fridges, pool.

$$$ Tropical Tambaú, Av Alm Tamandaré 229, T083-2107 1900, www.tropicalhotel. com.br. An enormous round building on the seafront which looks like a rocket- launching station and has comfortable motel-style rooms around its perimeter. Good service. Recommended.

$$$ Victory Business Flat, Av Tamandaré 310, T083-3041 3011, www.victoryflat.com.br. Furnished apartments with a pool and sauna. Cheaper in low season.

$$$ Xênius, Av Cabo Branco 1262, T083-3015 3519, www.xeniushotel.com.br. Popular standard 4-star hotel with a pool, good restaurant. Well-kept but standard a/c rooms, low-season reductions.

$$ Pouso das Águas, Av Cabo Branco 2348, Cabo Branco, T083-3226 5103. A homely atmosphere with landscaped areas and a pool.

$$ Solar Filipéia, Av Incognito Coracão de Jesus 153, T083-3219 3744, www.solarfilipeia. com.br. A recently opened, smart hotel with large, bright rooms with bathrooms in tile and black marble and excellent service. Good value.

$$ Tambía Praia, R Carlos Alverga 36, T083-3247 4101, www.tambiahotel.hpg.com.br. Centrally located and 1 block from the beach. Intimate, with balconies and sea view. Recommended.

$$ Villa Mare Apartment Hotel, Av Négo 707, T083-3226 2142. Comfortable apartments for 2 or 3 people with full amenities per night or from US$400-500 per month. Helpful staff. Recommended.

$ Hostel Manaíra, R Major Ciraulo 380, Manaíra, T083-3247 1962, www.manaira hostel.br2.net. Friendly new hostel close to the beach, with a pool, internet, barbecue, cable TV and breakfast. A real bargain.

$ Pousada Mar Azul, Av João Maurício 315, T083-3226 2660. Very clean large rooms, the best are on the upper level, on the oceanfront road. Some have a/c and private bath, others have fans. Well kept, safe and a real bargain.

Camping
Camping Clube do Brasil, Praia de Seixas, 13 km from the centre, T083-3247 2181.

Tambaba *p67*
$$ Chalé Suiço, R Chalé Suiço 120, Tabatinga, T083-3981 2046. Small, shared bath, restaurant, upstairs rooms have ocean-view balconies.

$$ Jacuma's Lodge, PB008, T083-3290 1977, www.jacuma.tur.br. Very simple tiled a/c rooms decorated with lacey rugs, curtains and counterpanes sitting in a small hotel right on the beach. There's a pleasant shady pool area with tables, sun loungers and a paddling pool for children.

$$ Pousada Corais de Carapibus, Av Beira Mar, Carapebus, T083-3290 1179, www.coraisdecarapibus.com.br. A few kilometres south of Jacumã. With bath, pool, restaurant and a nice breeze since it is located on a cliff across from the ocean.

Campina Grande *p68*
Many hotels around Praça da Bandeira.

$$$ Garden, R Engenheiro José Bezerra 400, Mirante Km 5, T083-3310 4000, www.gardenhotelcampina.com. The vast hotel complex is Campina Grande's best hotel, sitting on a hill 5 km (3 miles) from the centre, with views out over the city. There are 5 swimming pools, a well-equipped gym, squash courts and aerobics classes. Rooms are vast and spartan, with verandas and all come with broadband internet.

$$ Mahatma Gandhi, Floriano Peixoto 338, T/F083-3321 5275. With bath, a/c, fridge.

$$ Pérola, Floriano Peixoto 258, T083-3341 5319. With bath and a/c, cheaper with fan, parking and a very good breakfast.

$$ Regente, Barão do Abiaí 80, T083-3321 3843. With bath, a/c or fan, fridge.

$$ Souto Maior, Floriano Peixoto 289, T083-3321 8043. Rooms include bath a/c and fridge.

$$ Village, R Octacílio Nepomuceno 1285, Catole, Rodoviária Nova 4km, T083-3310 8000, www.hoteisvillage.com.br. This large business hotel is in a good location near the shopping centre mall and is equipped with tennis courts swimming pools, hot tubs and a spa.

$ Aurora, 7 de Setembro 120, T083-3321 4874. Shared bath, very basic and run down.

$ Avenida, Floriano Peixoto 378, T083- 3341 1249. With fan, good value, cheaper with shared bath.

$ Eliu's, Maciel Pinheiro 31B, 1st floor, T083-3321 4115. Clean, friendly, a/c and bath (cheaper with fan/without bath), good value.

$ Verona, 13 de Maio 232, T083-3341 1926. With bath, fan, good value, friendly service.

Cariri *p69*
A visit to **Fazenda Pai Mateus**, www.pai mateus.com.br, can be organized through **Cariri Ecotours**, see page 89.

$$ Dormitório Sertanejo I, R Col Zé

Vicente, Cariri. Rooms nice and clean with bath and fan. No breakfast, but good value. Recommended.

$$ Gadelha Palace, Trav Luciana Rocha 2, Cariri, T081-3521 1416. With bath, a/c, fridge, pool and restaurant.

$ Dormitório Aguiar, R João Gualberto, Cariri. Very basic.

🍴 Eating

João Pessoa *p64, maps p64 and p66*
There are few eating options in the city centre. Locals eat at the stalls in **Parque Solon de Lucena** next to the lake, where there are a couple of simple restaurants.

Urban beaches *p65, map p66*
Every evening on the beachfront, stalls sell all kinds of snacks and barbecued meats. At **Cabo Branco** there are many straw huts on the beach serving cheap eats and seafood.

♔♔♔ Adega do Alfredo, Coração de Jesus. Very popular traditional Portuguese restaurant in the heart of the club and bar area.

♔♔♔ Gulliver, Av Olinda 590, Tambaú. Trendy French/Brazilian restaurant frequented by João Pessoa's middle classes.

♔♔ Cheiro Verde, R Carlos Alverga 43. Self-service, well established, regional food.

♔♔ Mangaí, Av General Édson Ramalho 696, Manaíra, T083-3226 1615. This is one of the best restaurants in the northeast to sample the region's cooking. There are almost 100 different hot dishes to chose from, sitting in copper tureens over a traditional wood-fired stove some 20 m long. The open-sided dining area is very welcoming and spacious. Very good Italian too with a charming atmosphere.

♔♔ Sapore d'Italia, Av Cabo Branco 1584, Standard Italian fare including pizza.

Campina Grande *p68*
Rua 13 de Maio by Rui Barbosa in the centre has several good restaurants. There are many

bars near **Parque do Povo**, busy at weekends.

¥¥ **A Cabana do Possidônio**, 13 de Maio 207 T083-3341 3384. A varied menu of regional and international dishes.

¥¥ **La Nostra Casa**, R 13 de Maio 175, T083-3322 5196. Modest but friendly pasta and pizza restaurant.

¥ **Carne & Massa**, R 13 de Maio 214, T083-3322 8677. Regional cooking including *carne de sol*, pasta and a range of desserts.

¥ **La Suissa**, Dep João Tavares 663. Good savoury and sweet snacks.

¥ **Lanchonette Casa das Frutas**, Marquês de Herval 54. Good-value meals, fruit juices and snacks.

¥ **Manoel da Carne de Sol**, Félix de Araújo 263. T083-3321 2877. One of the city's best-value regional restaurants including an excellent *carne de sol* lunch with runner beans, *farofa* manioc flour and vegetables.

¥ **Vila Antiga**, R 13 de Maio 164, T083-3341 4718. A popular pay by weight restaurant with a broad range of regional dishes, pastas, salads and desserts.

Souza *p70*
Several restaurants are on R Col Zé Vicente.
¥ **Diagonal**, Getúlio Vargas 2. Ordinary but reasonable pizzeria.

🎵 Bars and clubs

João Pessoa *p64, maps p64 and p66*
There are many open bars on and across from the beach in Tambaú and Cabo Branco; the area known as **Feirinha de Tambaú**, on Av Tamandaré by the Tambaú Hotel and nearby streets, sees much movement even on weekend nights, with **R Coração do Jesus** being the epicentre. There are numerous little bars and *forró* places here and this is the place for a night-time browse. Other beachfront neighbourhoods also have popular bars.
Fashion Club, Mega Shopping, Manaíra.

The most popular nightclub in the city, with a 20-something crowd and mostly techno and MPB. Large beachfront *baracca* restaurant with live music at weekends.

Incognito, R Coração do Jesus. A very popular and lively bar and dance club. There are many others here including **KS**.

Mr Caipira, Av João Maurício 1533, Manaíra, T083-246 7597. Live acoustic music, Brazilian barbecued food, *feijoada* and a smart 30-something crowd. On the seafront road.

Zodiaco, Incognito Coração do Jesus 144. One of several nightclubs in the area attracting a lively young crowd especially at the weekends.

❀ Festivals and events

João Pessoa *p64, maps p64 and p66*
Feb Pre-carnival celebrations in João Pessoa are renowned: the *bloco* **Acorde Miramar** opens the celebrations the Tue before Carnaval. On Wed, known as **Quarta Feira de Fogo**, thousands join the **Muriçocas de Miramar**, forming a *bloco* second only to Recife's **Galo da Madrugada** with as many as 300,000 people taking part.

5 Aug The street celebrations for the patroness of the city, **Nossa Senhora das Neves**, last for 10 days to the rhythm of *frevo*.

Campina Grande *p68*
Apr **Micarande**, the out-of-season Salvador-style carnival.

Jun-Jul Campina Grande boasts the largest São João celebrations in Brazil; from the beginning of Jun into the 1st week of Jul the city attracts many visitors; there are bonfires and *quadrilhas* (square dance groups) in every neighbourhood; *forró* and invited artists at the Parque do Povo; *quentão*, *pomonha* and *canjica* are consumed everywhere.

Aug The annual **Congresso de Violeiros**, which gathers singers and guitarists from all across the northeast.

○ Shopping

João Pessoa *p64, maps p64 and p66*
Cheaper arts and crafts can be bought at
Mercado de Artesanato, Centro de Turismo,
Almte Tamandaré 100, Tambaú, daily
0800-1800; **Mercados de Artesanato
Paraibano**, Av Rui Carneiro, Tambaú, daily
0900-1700; **Bosque dos Sonhos**, by the Cabo
Branco lighthouse. Weekends only.
Terra do Sol, R Coração do Jesus 145, T083-
3226 1940, www.terradosol.art.br. The best
place to buy regional crafts, including lace,
embroidery and ceramics. Very elegant, high-
quality bedspreads, bath robes, hammocks
and tablecloths made from natural cotton.
Also sells work by Paraíba artists and artisans.

▲ Activities and tours

João Pessoa *p64, maps p64 and p66*
Cliotur, Av Alm Tamandaré 310, Sala 2,
T083-3247 4460. Trips to the *sertão*. Also
offers light adventure activities.
Roger Turismo, Av Tamandaré 229, T083-
3247 1856. Half-day city tours (US$6), day
trips to Tambaba (US$8) and Recife/Oldina
(US$12). A large agency with some English-
speaking guides and a range of other tours.

Excursions from João Pessoa *p66*
Flaviano Gouveia, Jacaré, T083-3982 1604.
Ultralight aircraft rides, US$19 for 8-min ride
or US$115 for 1 hr.
Sea Tech, PO Box 42, João Pessoa, 56001-
970, T083-3245 1476. Run by Brian Ingram,
originally from England. Boatyard and
frequent port of call for international
yachtspeople plying the Brazilian coast.

⊖ Transport

João Pessoa *p64, maps p64 and p66*
Air A taxi to the airport costs US$8 from the
centre or US$12 from Tambaú. Flights to **São
Paulo**, **Brasília**, **Recife** and **Rio de Janeiro**.
Gol flies to **São Paulo** or **Rio** from Recife, and
provides free bus transport from João Pessoa.

Airline offices **Avianca**, www.Avianca.
com.br. **GOL**, www.voegol.com.br, and at
the airport. **TAM**, T083-3247 2400, Av
Senador Rui Carneiro 512, T083-3247 2400.
Bus From the *rodoviária* or Lagoa (Parque
Solon de Lucena), take bus No 510 for
Tambaú, No 507 for **Cabo Branco**.

Buses to **Recife** with Boa Vista or
Bonfim, every 30 mins, US$2.50, 2 hrs. To
Natal with Nordeste, every 2 hrs, US$8
convencional, US$7.50 *executivo*, 3 hrs. To
Fortaleza with Nordeste, 2 daily, 10 hrs,
US$18. To **Campina Grande** with Real,
every 30 mins, US$4, 2 hrs. To **Juazeiro do
Norte** with Transparaíba, 2 daily, US$14,
10 hrs. To **Salvador** with Progresso, 4
weekly, US$30, 14 hrs. To **Brasília** via
Campina Grande, with Planalto, 2 weekly,
US$57, 48 hrs. To **Rio de Janeiro** with São
Geraldo, daily, US$67 *convencional*, US$80
executivo, 42 hrs. To **São Paulo** with
Itapemirim, daily, US$73 *convencional*,
US$76 *executivo*, 47 hrs. To **Belém** with
Guanabara, daily, US$46, 36 hrs.

Car hire **Avis**, Av Nossa Senhora dos
Navegantes, 402, T083-3247 3050. **Localiza**,
Av Epitácio Pessoa 4910, T083-3247 4030,
and at the airport, T0800-992000. **Tempo**,
Almte Tamandaré 100, at the Centro de
Turismo, T083-3247 0002.

Train Regional services west to **Bayeux** and
Santa Rita, and **Cabedelo** in the north.

Tambaba *p67*
Bus From Tambaba a dirt road leads 12 km
north to the beach of **Jacumã**, from where the
PB-018 goes 11 km west to **Conde** and
continues 3 km to the BR-101, which runs 20 km
north to **João Pessoa**. There are hourly buses
from Jacumã to **João Pessoa** 0530-1900.

Campina Grande *p68*
Air Daily flights to **Recife** with Nordeste.
Taxi to airport US$7. City bus Distrito

The world's greatest barn dance – the Festas Juninas

Carnaval is essentially an urban, black Brazilian celebration. The Festas Juninas, which take place throughout Brazil during June, are a rural celebration. While carnival pounds to samba, the Juninhas pulsate to the triangle and accordion of *forró*. Rather than wearing feathers and sequins, Juninas revellers dress up as *caipiras* (yokels) in tartan shirts and reed hats; and they eat *canjica* (maize porridge) and drink *quentão* (a Brazilian version of mulled wine). And they do it in enormous numbers. During the most important weekend of the festivals – the eve of St John's Day on 23 June – over one million mock-*caipiras* descend on the little backland towns of Campina Grande in Paraíba and Caruaru in Pernambuco. Both towns are entirely taken over by *forró* bands, cowboys, stalls selling *doce de leite* and other country produce, and the percussion of fireworks and bangers. Foreign visitors are still a rare curiosity.

Industrial from Praça Clementino Procópio, behind Cine Capitólio.

Bus To **João Pessoa**, with **Real**, every 30 mins, US$3, 2 hrs. To **Souza** with Transparaíba, 6 daily, US$7, 6 hrs. To **Juazeiro do Norte** with Transparaíba, 2 daily, US$10, 9 hrs. To **Natal** with Nordeste, 0800 daily, US$6, 18 hrs. To **Rio** with Itapemirim, 1600 daily, US$65, 42 hrs. To **Brasília** with Planalto, 2 weekly, US$55, 46 hrs.

Car hire On R Tavares Cavalcante are **Intermezzo**, No 27, T083-321 4790; **Kelly's**, No 301, T/F083-3322 4539. Also **Localiza**, R Dr Severino Cruz 625, T083-3341 4034, and at the airport, T083-3331 4594.

Souza *p70*
Bus To **Campina Grande** with Transparaíba, 6 daily, US$7, 6 hrs. To **João Pessoa** with Transparaíba, 6 daily, US$10, 8 hrs. To **Juazeiro or Boa Esperança** with Transparaíba, 4 daily, US$4, 3½ hrs. To **Mossoró**, RN, with Jardinense, 4 daily, US$6, 4½ hrs.

❶ Directory

João Pessoa *p64, maps p64 and p66*
Banks Banco 24 horas, Av Almirante Tamandaré 100, Tambaú, ATM for Cirrus, Visa and MasterCard. **Banco do Brasil**, Praça 1817, 3rd floor, Centro, Isidro Gomes 14, Tambaú, behind Centro de Turismo. **HSBC**, R Peregrino de Carvalho, 162, Centre, ATM for cirrus and visa. **Mondeo Tour**, Av Négo 46, Tambaú, T083-3226 3100. 0900- 1730, cash and Tcs. **PB Câmbio Turismo**, Visconde de Pelotas 54C, Centro, Mon-Fri 1030-1630, cash and TCs. **Internet** **Cyberpointy Café**, Av Almirante Tamandaré, 100, in Centro Turístico Tambaú, daily 0800-2100, US1.60 per hr. **Post office** Main office is at Praça Pedro Américo, Varadouro; central office is at Parque Solon de Lucena 375; also by the beach at Av Rui Carneiro, behind the Centro de Turismo. **Telephone** Calling stations at: Visconde de Pelotas and Miguel Couto, Centro; Centro de Turismo, Tambaú; Av Epitácio Pessoa 1487, Bairro dos Estados; *rodoviária* and airport.

Campina Grande *p68*
Banks Banco do Brasil, 7 de Setembro 52, cash and TCs at poor rates. **Mondeo Tour**, R Índios Cariris 308, cash at good rates and TCs, Mon-Fri 1000-1600. **Post office** R Marquês do Herval, Praça da Bandeira. **Telephone** Floriano Peixoto 410 by Praça da Bandeira in the industrial district and at the *rodoviária*.

Contents

At a glance

◎ **Getting around** Bus and internal flights. Car hire is not recommended as roads can be poor and badly signposted, especially in the interior.

⟳ **Time required** 1 day for Fortaleza; 2-3 days for São Luís and Alcântara; 2-3 days for the Lençóis Maranhenses; 10 days for the whole region.

☁ **Weather** Hot and wet Jan-Jun, hot and dry Jul-Dec.

⊗ **When not to go** Mar and Apr have the most rain and least sunshine.

Fortaleza and the far northeast

Rio Grande do Norte

This state is famous for its beaches and dunes, especially around Natal. The coastline begins to change here, becoming gradually drier and less green, as it shifts from running north–south to east–west. The vast sugar cane plantations and few remaining stands of Mata Atlântica (coastal forest) are replaced by the dry caatinga vegetation and caju orchards. The people are known as 'Potiguares', after an indigenous tribe that once resided in the state.

»» For listings, see pages 84-91.

Natal and around → For listings, see pages 84-91. Phone code: 084. Population: 713,000.

The state capital, located on a peninsula between the Rio Potengi and the Atlantic Ocean, is pleasant enough but has few sights of interest. Most visitors head for the beaches to the north and south. During the Second World War, the city was, somewhat bizarrely, the second largest US base outside the United States and housed 8000 American pilots.

Ins and outs

Getting there Flights arrive at **Augusto Severo International Airport** ① *Parnamirim, 18 km south of centre, 10 km from Ponta Negra, T084-3644 1070,* from Belém, Brasília, Fernando de Noronha, Fortaleza, Recife, Rio de Janeiro, Salvador and São Paulo. A taxi to the centre costs US$25; US$20 to Ponta Negra. Buses run every 30 minutes to the old *rodoviária* near the centre, US$1 from where there are connections to Ponta Negra on route 54 or 56 amongst others, or take the 'Aeroporto' bus to the city centre and then bus Nos 54 or 46 south to Ponta Negra.

Interstate buses arrive at the new **Rodoviária Cidade do Sol** ① *Av Capitão Mor Gouveia 1237, Cidade da Esperança, 6 km southwest of the centre, T084-3205 4377.* A taxi to Ponta Negra costs around US$18; to the Via Costeira around US$25. Alternatively, take bus No 66 to Ponta Negra. This passes close to the hotel strip whilst not taking Avenida Erivan Franca (the street that runs along the seafront). For Praia do Meio beach and the Via Costeira take bus No 40 and alight at Praia do Meio for an easy walk to any of the hotels on that beach or Praia dos Artistas. Or take any of the Via Costeira buses.

Buses from the south pass Ponta Negra first, where you can ask to alight. The city buses 'Cidade de Esperança Avenida 9', 'Areia Preta via Petrópolis' or 'Via Tirol' run from the new *rodoviária* to the centre. It is also possible to travel between Natal and Fortaleza by beach buggy: an exciting trip but not a very environmentally responsible one as buggies have seriously eroded the coast. »» See Transport, page 90.

Getting around Unlike most Brazilian buses, in Natal you get on the bus at the front and get off at the back. The **Old Rodoviária** ① *Av Junqueira Aires, by Praça Augusto Severo, Ribeira,* is a central point where many bus lines converge. Buses to some of the nearby

Natal

Natal orientation

Sleeping 🛏
Bruma 4
Imirá Plaza 2
Maine 3
Porto Mirim 5

Eating 🍴
A Macrobiótica 1
Raro Sabor 2

N
Not to scale

beaches also leave from here. Taxis are expensive compared to other cities (eg four times the price of Recife); a typical 10-minute journey costs US$15. Buses are the best option. Route 54 and 46 connect Ponta Negra with the city, the former via Via Costeira and the old *rodoviária*.

Tourist information The state tourist office, SETUR ① *Centro de Turismo R Aderbal de Figueiredo 980, Petrópolis, T084-3211 5013 www.setur.rn.gov.brwww.rosaleao.com.br/clientes/setur*, covers the whole of Rio Grande do Norte state, although their information and English is very limited, and the office is not conveniently located. However, there are **tourist information booths** at the airport, the bus station, on Avenida Presidente Café Filho on Praia das Artistas beach and Erivan Franca on Ponta Negra, all open daily 0800-2100. See www.natal trip.com, www.natal.com.br and www.rn. gov.br for more information.

Sights

No-one comes to Natal for sightseeing, but the city is not without culture. The oldest part is the **Ribeira** along the riverfront, where a programme of renovation has been started. This can be seen on Rua Chile and in public buildings restored in vivid art deco fashion, such as the **Teatro Alberto Maranhão** ① *Praça Agusto Severo, T/F084-3222 9935*, built 1898-1904, and the **Prefeitura** ① *R Quintino Bocaiuva, Cidade Alta*. The **Cidade Alta**, or Centro, is the main commercial centre and Avenida Rio Branco its principal artery. The main square is made up by the adjoining *praças*, **João Maria**, **André de Albuquerque**, **João Tibúrcio** and **7 de Setembro**. At Praça André de Albuquerque is the old **cathedral** (inaugurated 1599, restored 1996). The modern cathedral is on Avenida Deodoro. The church of **Santo Antônio** ① *R Santo Antônio 683, Cidade Alta, Tue-Fri 0800-1700*,

Sat 0800-1400, dates from 1766, and has a fine, carved wooden altar and a sacred art museum.

The **Museu Câmara Cascudo** ⓘ *Av Hermes de Fonseca 1440, Tirol, T084-3212 2795, www.mcc.ufrn.br, Tue-Fri 0800-1130, 1400-1730, Sat, Sun 1300-1700, US$2.50*, has exhibits on *umbanda* rituals, archaeological digs, the sugar, leather and petroleum industries; there is also a dead whale.

The 16th-century **Forte dos Reis Magos** ⓘ *T084-3202 9006, daily 0800-1630, US$1.50*, is at Praia do Forte, the tip of Natal's peninsula. Between the fort and the city is a military installation. Walk along the beach to the fort for good views (or go on a tour, or by taxi).

At Mãe Luiza is a **lighthouse** with beautiful views of Natal and surrounding beaches (take a city bus marked 'Mãe Luiza' and get the key from the house next door).

South to Ponta Negra

The urban beaches of **Praia do Meio**, **Praia dos Artistas** and **Praia de Areia Preta** have recently been cleaned up. The first two are sheltered by reefs and good for windsurfing. The beachside promenade, **Via Costeira**, runs south beneath the towering sand dunes of **Parque das Dunas** (access restricted to protect the dunes), joining the city to the neighbourhood of Ponta Negra. A cycle path parallels this road and provides great views of the coastline.

The vibrant and pretty **Ponta Negra**, 12 km south of the centre (20 minutes by bus), is justifiably the most popular beach and has many hotels. The northern end is good for surfing, while the southern end is calmer and suitable for swimming. **Morro do Careca**, a 120-m-high sand dune, surrounded by vegetation, sits at its far end. It is crowded on weekends and holidays. The poorly lit northern reaches can be unsafe after dark.

Excursions from Natal

The beautiful beaches around Natal – some of which are developed, others are deserted

Ponta Negra

Sleeping
Albergue da Costa **15**
Caminho do Mar **5**
HI Lua Cheia **12**
Ingá Praia **6**

Manary Praia **1**
Ocean Paláce **14**
O Tempo e o Vento **4**
Pousada América do Sol **10**
Pousada Maravista **11**

Pousada Porta do Sol **9**
Praia Azul Mar **2**
Verdes Mares **13**

Not to scale

and accessible only by trails – are good all year round for day trips or longer stays. Those north of the city are known as the **Litoral Norte**, where there are extensive cashew plantations; those to the south form the **Litoral Sul**. The areas closest to the city are built-up and get busy during the summer holidays (December to Carnaval), when dune-buggy traffic can become excessive.

Popular tours from Natal include boat trips on the **Rio Potengi**, along the nearby beaches of the Litoral Sul, and to **Barra do Cunhaú**, 86 km south of Natal. The latter goes through mangroves and visits an island and a salt mine, **Passeio Ecológico Cunhaú** ⓘ *T084-9934 0017, www.barradocunhau.com.br*. Other popular pastimes include buggy tours, marlin fishing (11 km from shore, said by some to be the best in Brazil) and microlight flights over the Rio Potengi and sand dunes north of Natal.▶▶ *See Activities and tours, page 89.*

The **Centro de Lançamento da Barreira do Inferno** ⓘ *11 km south of Natal on the road to Pirangi, T084-3216 1400, www.clbi.cta.br, visits by appointment on Wed from 1400*, is the launching centre for Brazil's space programme.

Southern coast → *For listings, see pages 84-91.*

South of Natal, the Rota do Sol/Litoral Sul (RN-063) follows the coastline for some 55 km and provides access to beaches south of Ponta Negra. From here the coast becomes more remote and long curves of white sand backed by multicoloured sandstone cliffs and sweeping dunes, fragments of Atlantic forest alive with rare birds, black tea lagoons and bays filled with dolphins, make this one of the most popular stretches in the northeast. Thankfully development is small scale and it still feels relaxed (outside high season). Several species of turtles, including giant leatherbacks, still nest here, although numbers are declining as the popularity of beach buggy tourism grows. The best place to stay along this stretch of coast is **Pipa**, a lively little town with good *pousadas* and restaurants.

Ins and outs
Buses run along Litoral Sul from both Natal's bus stations, every 30 minutes in summer, stopping at **Pirangi** (US$4, one hour), and **Tabatinga** (US$5, 1¼ hours); there are six daily buses to **Tibau** and **Pipa** (two to three hours).

From João Pessoa in Paraíba you will have to change at Goaianinha on the main road to Natal. This route is also run by *combis*, which leave when full up and cost about 20% more than the buses. *Combis* connect Pipa and Tibau until around 2300.

Rota do Sol
Praia do Cotovelo, 21 km from Natal, offers a view of the Barreira do Inferno rocket-launching centre to the north. At its southern end it has some cliffs and coconut palms where camping is possible.

Pirangi do Norte, 25 km from Natal (30 minutes by bus) has calm waters and is popular for watersports and offshore bathing (500 m out) when natural pools form between the reefs. Nearby is the world's largest *cajueiro* (cashew tree); branches springing from a single trunk cover 7300 sq m. The snack bar by the tree has schedules of buses back to Natal. Lacemakers offer bargains for clothing and tableware. Pirangi has a lively **Carnaval**.

Búzios, 35 km from Natal, has a pleasant setting with vegetation-covered dunes and coconut palms. The water is mostly calm and clear, making it good for bathing.

Barra de Tabatinga, 45 km from Natal, is surrounded by cliffs used for parasailing. Waves are strong here, making it a popular surfing beach. A new 'shark park' complete with resident biologist is its latest attraction.

Camurupim and **Barreta**, 46 km and 55 km from Natal respectively, have reefs near the shore, where bathing pools form at low tide; this area has many restaurants specializing in shrimp. Beyond Barreta is the long, pristine beach of **Malenbar** or **Guaraíra**, accessible on foot or on a 10-minute boat ride across the Rio Tibau. Buggy tours from Natal cost US$100.

Tibau do Sul and Pipa → *Population 6124.*

The little fishing town of **Tibau do Sul** has cobbled streets and sits high on a cliff between surf beaches and the manatee-filled Lago de Guaraíra. Boat trips can be arranged from here to the *lago* or to see dolphins in the calm waters offshore. Although most tourists head straight for Pipa, which is more developed, the beach *barracas* in Tibau are lively at night with *forró* and MPB. Natal's finest restaurants are also here (see Eating, page 87) and there are a handful of decent *pousadas* in town.

From Tibau, a series of white-sand crescents, separated by rocky headlands and backed by high cliffs crowned with coconut groves and remnant coastal forest, stretches south to **Pipa**. This is one of Natal's most enchanting little tourist towns, whose mix of local fishermen and settlers from all over Brazil has formed an eclectic alternative community. There are excellent *pousadas* and restaurants in all price ranges and the nightlife is animated. The town is becoming increasingly popular and the number of people can feel overwhelming during Carnaval and New Year.

The town beach is somewhat developed, but there are plenty of others nearby. **Praia dos Golfinhos** to the south and **Madeiro** beyond it have only a few hotels and **Praia do Amor** to the north is surrounded by cliffs and has reasonable surf. Access to the shore is down the steps built by the few clifftop hotels or by walking along the beach from Pipa at low tide. There are tours to see dolphins from US$10 per person and also around the mangrove-lined **Lagoa Guaraíra** at Tibau, particularly beautiful at sunset.

Just north of town, on a 70-m-high dune, is the **Santuário Ecológico de Pipa** ① *T084-3211 6070, www.pipa.com.br/santuarioecologico, 0800-1600, US$3,* a 60-ha park created in 1986 to conserve the *Mata Atlântica* forest. There are several trails and lookouts over the cliffs, which afford an excellent view of the ocean and dolphins. Although larger animals like cats and howler monkeys are long gone, this is one of the few areas in the state where important indicator bird species, such as guans, can be found.

Genipabu and the northern coast → *For listings, see pages 84-91.*

The coast north of Natal is known for its many impressive, light-coloured sand dunes, some reaching a staggering 50 m in height. **Genipabu**, a weekend resort for the Natal middle classes, is the most of these and is only a very short bus ride from the city. The country beyond the resort is well off the tourist trail, with vast long beaches backed by multicoloured cliffs, dunes and salt lakes. It is dramatic terrain, so much so that it has been used as the backdrop to numerous biblical films. Three crosses stand over the cliffs at **Areia Branca**, left there by one of the most recent productions, *Maria, A Mãe do Filho de Deus*. The best way to experience the majesty of the coastal landscape is to walk and listen to the wind on the sand. Buggy tourism has led to the degradation of many of the northeast's dunes. Fixed dunes are protected and should not be disturbed, but shifting dunes can be visited by buggy, camel or horse. Ask locally for advice.

Ins and outs

Areia Branca and the other small towns along the northern coast are reachable from Mossoró, the second largest town in the state but with little in the way of tourist attractions. Galinhos, in the far north, sits on a long broad sandspit and is connected to the mainland by ferry from the little village of Guamaré. From here, there are buses to both Mossoró and Natal via the small town of Jandaíra.

Redinha

A 25-minute ferry crossing on the Rio Potengi or a 16-km drive from Natal up the Rota do Sol/Litoral Norte, takes you to Redinha, an urban beach with ocean and river bathing and buggies for hire. The local delicacy is fried fish with tapioca, served at the market. About 5 km north of Redinha, on a point, is **Santa Rita**. From its high dunes there is a great view of the surrounding coastline.

Genipabu and around

The best-known beach in the state, Genipabu, is 30 km north of Natal. Its major attractions are some very scenic dunes and the **Lagoa de Genipabu**, a lake surrounded by cashew trees where tables are set up on a shoal in the water and drinks are served. There are also many bars and restaurants on the seashore. Buggy rental and microlight flights can be arranged. ▶ *See Activities and tours, page 90.*

North of Genipabu, across the Rio Ceará Mirim, are several beaches with coconut groves and dunes, lined with fishing villages and summer homes of people from Natal; access is via the town of Extremoz. One of these beaches, **Pitangui**, 35 km from Natal, is 6 km long and has a crystalline lake where colourful schools of fish can be seen. **Jacumã**, 49 km from Natal, has a small waterfall and the inland Lagoa de Jacumã, a lake surrounded by dunes where sand-skiing is popular.

Muriú, 44 km from Natal, is known for its lovely green ocean where numerous small boats and *jangadas* anchor; the beach has attractive palms (buggy tour from Natal, including shifting dunes US$100). About 5 km to the north is **Prainha** or **Coqueiro**, a beautiful cove with many coconut palms and strong waves.

Lovely beaches continue along the state's coastline; as you get further away from Natal the beaches are more distant from the main highways and access is more difficult. Around 83 km north of Natal, in the centre of a region known for its coconuts and lobsters, is the ugly resort town of **Touros**. From here the coastline veers east–west.

Far north → *Phone code: 084.*

As the coast turns to the west, the terrain becomes more dramatic and bleak. Sheltered coves are replaced by vast beaches stretching in seemingly interminable broad curves. Behind them are pink, brown and red cliffs, or large expanses of dunes. Highlights are the sleepy little village of **Galinhos**, with its sand streets and beautiful, gentle beach washed by a calm sea, and the **Costa Branca** near the little fishing towns of **Areia Branca**, **Ponta do Mel** and **Rosadao**, where huge pink and white dunes converge behind magnificent long beaches.

Rio Grande do Norte listings

Natal and around *p78, map p79*
Economical hotels are easier to find in Natal
than at the outlying beaches or Ponta Negra,
but very few people stay here and what they
save by doing so is often spent on public
transport to and from the beaches.

The distinction between **Praia do Meio**
and **Praia dos Artistas** is often blurred. Most
hotels are on the beachfront **Av Pres Café
Filho**, the numbering of which is illogical.

The **Via Costeira** is a strip of enormous,
upmarket beachfront hotels, which are very
isolated, with no restaurants or shops within
easy walking distance.

$$$$ Maine, Av Salgado Filho 1741, Lagoa
Nova, T084-4005 5774, www.hotelmaine.
com.br. A business-orientated 4-star in a
concrete tower in Natal town, with
reasonable service and a restaurant.

$$$ Bruma, Av Pres Café Filho 1176, T/F084-
3202 4303, www.hotelbruma.com.br. A small,
family-run beachfront hotel with 25
balconied rooms around a little pool. Popular
with Brazilian families.

$$$ Imirá Plaza, Via Costeira 4077, Praia
Barreira d'Agua, T084-3211 4104,
www.imiraplaza.com.br. A vast, sprawling
package resort on the beach and with a pool
and tennis court. Popular with families.
Cheaper in low season.

$$$ Porto Mirim, Av Café Filho 682, Praia
dos Artistas, T084-3220 1600,
www.portomirim.com.br. A smart, modern
seafront hotel with spacious public areas but
small tiled rooms and little rooftop pool and
deck with nice views. Cheaper off season.

Ponta Negra *p80, map p80*
Ponta Negra is the ideal place to stay, with its
attractive beach and concentration of
restaurants. The most popular hotels are those
right on the beach, on **Av Erivan França** facing

the sea, and on **R Francisco Gurgel** behind
that street. The latter is quieter.

$$$$ Manary Praia, R Francisco Gurgel
9067, T/F084-3204 2900,
www.manary.com.br. The best and most
tranquil hotel facing the beach and the only
one with a trace of style. The rooms, which
are decorated in hardwood and pastel
colours, have ample bathrooms and secluded
private terraces. Good food. A **Roteiros de
Charme** hotel, see page 10.

$$$$ Ocean Paláce, Km 11, near Ponta
Negra, T084-3220 4144,
www.oceanpalace.com.br. A 5-star with
large, comfortable suites, smaller, pokier
family rooms and a string of bungalows in a
regimented line near the beach. Public areas
include a lovely ocean-front pool and terrace.
Relaxed and friendly.

$$$ Hotel e Pousada O Tempo e o Vento,
R Elias Barros 66, T/F084-3219 2526,
www.otempoeovento.com.br. Small
terracotta and whitewash hotel a block back
from the beach with a range of a/c rooms
gathered around a pool. The *luxo* rooms are
by far the best, others have a fan and there
are low season discounts.

$$$ Praia Azul Mar, R Franscisco Gurgel 92,
T084-4005 3555, www.praia-azul.com.
Pleasant and well-run package holiday hotel,
with a/c rooms and a pool over-looking the
beach.

$$ Caminho do Mar, R Dr Ernani Hugo
Gomes 365, T084-3219 3761. Simple plain
rooms and breakfast, a short walk from the
beach.

$$ Ingá Praia, Av Erivan França 17,
T084-3219 3436,
www.ingapraiahotel.com.br. A pink cube on
the beach with comfortable well-kept rooms
and a rooftop terrace. Wi-Fi in all rooms.

$$ Pousada América do Sol, R Erivan
França 35, T084-3219 2245, www.pousada
americadosol.com.br. Very simple a/c rooms

with pokey bathrooms and TVs. Good breakfast in a terrace overlooking the beach and substantial off-season reductions.

$$ Pousada Porta do Sol, R Erivan França 9057, T084-3236 2555, www.pousadaporta dosol.com.br. Basic rooms with TV, fridge, fan and an excellent breakfast, pool, beachfront, good value.

$ Albergue da Costa, Av Praia de Ponta Negra 8932, T084-3219 0095, www.albergue dacosta.com.br. A simple hostel in a great location, with public areas strewn with hammocks and with rather scruffy little rooms and dorms. The low prices are per person.

$ HI Lua Cheia, R Dr Manoel Augusto Bezerra de Araújo 500, T084-3236 3696, www.luacheia.com.br. One of the best youth hostels in Brazil; in a 'castle' with a 'medieval' **Taverna Pub** in the basement. The price includes breakfast.

$ Pousada Maravista, R da Praia 223, T084-3236 4677, http://maravistabrasil.com. Plain and simple but with a good breakfast, English spoken, TV, fridge.

$ Verdes Mares, R das Algas 2166, Conj Algamar, T084-3236 2872, www.hostel verdesmares.com.br. HI youth hostel, price pp, includes breakfast, discount in low season.

Rota do Sol p81

$$ Pousada Esquina do Sol, Av Deputado Márcio Marinho 2210, Pirangi do Norte, T084-3238 2078, www.esquinadosol.com.br. Small hotel a stroll form the beach with a range of fan-cooled and a/c rooms and kitchenettes in a low-rise concrete block with verandas. Small pool and generous breakfast.

$$ Varandas de Búzios, Av Beira Mar s/n, Búzios, T084-3239 2121, www.rcentrium.com/cl/varandasbuzios. Regimented rows of cabins and a large central restaurant and public area with a pool right on the beach. Reasonable restaurant.

Tibau do Sul and Pipa p82

In Pipa more than 30 *pousadas* and many private homes offer accommodation.

$$$$ Ponta do Madeiro, R da Praia, Estr para Pipa Km 3, T/F084-3246 4220, www.pontado madeiro.com.br. Very comfortable spacious a/c chalets, beautiful pool with bar and spectacular views over the Praia do Madeiro. Excellent service and a good restaurant. Highly recommended.

$$$$ Sombra e Água Fresca, Praia do Amor, T084-3246 2144, www.sombraeagua fresca.com.br. Cheaper in low season. Tastefully decorated but small chalet rooms and vast luxury suites with separate sitting and dining areas. All with magnificent views.

$$$$ Toca da Coruja, Praia da Pipa, T084-3246 2226, www.tocadacoruja.com.br. One of the best small luxury hotels in north-eastern Brazil, with a range of chalets set in forested gardens and decorated with north-east Brazilian antiques and art. Beautiful pool and an excellent restaurant. A member of the **Roteiros de Charme** group, see page 10.

$$$$ Village Natureza, Canto do Madeiro, Pipa, T/F084-3246 4200, www.villagenatureza. com.br. Beautifully appointed a/c chalets nestled in tropical wooded gardens overlooking the sea and Madeiro beach. Gorgeous circular pool, pleasant grounds, lovely views and a long series of steep steps leading to the beach.

$$$ Marinas Tibau Sul, Tibau do Sul, T/F084-3246 4111, www.hotelmarinas. com.br. Cabins for 4, pool, restaurant, watersports, horse riding and a boat dock.

$$$ Mirante de Pipa, R do Mirante 1, Praia da Pipa, T084-3246 2055, www.mirante depipa.com.br. A/c and fan-cooled chalets with a veranda set in a forested garden. Wonderful views.

$$ A Conchego, R do Ceu s/n, Praia da Pipa, T084-3246 2439, www.pousada-aconchego. com. Family-run *pousada* with simple chalets with red-tiled roofs and terraces, in a garden filled with cashew and palm trees. Tranquil and central. Good breakfast.

$ Pousada da Pipa, Praia da Pipa, T084-3246 2271, www.pipa.com.br/pousada dapipa.com. Small rooms decorated with a personal touch. The best are upstairs and have a large shared terrace with glazed terracotta tiles, sitting areas and hammocks. Large breakfast.

$ Vera-My house, Praia da Pipa, T084-3246 2295, www.praiadapipa.com/veramyhouse. Good value, friendly and well maintained though simple rooms with bath, **$** per person in dormitory, use of kitchen, no breakfast. Recommended.

Camping
Eco-Camping da Pipa, Av Baía dos Golfinhos 10a, Praia da Pipa, T084-3222 0432/9413 5337, www.ecopipa.com. Great full-powered campsite with cooking facilities, showers and cabins (**$**) for those who don't want to use a tent. Right near Golfinhos beach.

Genipabu and the northern coast *p83*
$$$ Genipabu, Estr de Genipabu s/n, 2 km from beach, T084-3225 2063, www.genipabu.com. br/portugues. A very relaxing spa hotel on a hillside outside of town with wonderful views out over the beaches and sea. Smart and very well-kept a/c rooms with en suites. Treatments include Ayurvedic massage, reiki, yoga, body wraps and facials, see www.spanaturalis. com.br. Attractive pool and a sauna. Sister hotel on the beach, **Peixe Galo**, www.pousadapeixegalo.com.br.

$$ do Gostoso, Praia Ponta de Santo Cristo, 27 km west of town, T084-3263 4087, www.pousadadogostoso.com.br. Rustic chalets on a lonely stretch of beach and in the style of *sertão* houses. Simple restaurant.

$$ Pousada Villa do Sol, Enseada do Genipabu, Km 4, T084-3225 2132, www.villa dosol.com.br. 20 attractive a/c chalets, the best of which are the 5 newest, with views over the river. Small pool and restaurant with good service.

$$ Soleil, Av Beira Mar 91, Res Tabu, T084-3225 2064, www.pousadadosoleil.com.br. 10 simple rooms in a brightly painted *pousada* right on the beach. Facilities include a pool, a BBQ and internet.

Far north *p83*
There are plenty of *pousadas* in **Tibau** and many restaurants and bars along the beach. Although there are some *pousadas* in **Areia Branca**, it isn't a good base for the beaches. **Ponta do Mel**, which is flanked by 2 magnificent beaches, is better and has a couple of very basic *pousadas* in the town.

Galinhos town is very sleepy and *pousadas* often close up for a few days whilst their owners go away. There are at least 7 in town so it is always possible to find a room, either on the ocean or the coastal side.

$$$ Pousada Costa Branca, Ponta do Mel, Costa Branca, T084-3332 7062, www.costa branca.com.br. The best hotel between Genipabu and Ceará with a range of cabins on a bluff with magnificent views over an endless stretch of beach. Organized tours to the dunes to the south, which are among the most spectacular in the state. Good restaurant, service and pool, and Lord Byron tribute bar with live music.

$$ Chalé Oásis Galinhos, R Beira Rio s/n, Galinhos, T084-3552 0024, www.oasis galinhos.com. The best option in Galinhos, with 6 brightly painted a/c wooden chalets with palm-thatch roofs. All are individually decorated in lush pinks or cool blues, and come with wicker furnishings and arty bric-a-brac. Public areas are splashed with tropical colours and include a TV room lounge with comfy armchairs and a pool and sundeck overlooking the beach. The *pousada* organizes trips around Galinhos.

$ Panorama, Tibau, T084-3236 2208. Very basic rooms with a bath and more expensive options with fans.

$ Pousada e Restaurante Brasil Aventura, Galinhos, T084-3552 0085. One of several very simple beachfront *pousadas* with a fish restaurant. Plain but well kept and popular with backpackers.

🍴 Eating

Natal and south to Ponta Negra *p78, map p79*

Prawns feature heavily on menus as Natal is the largest exporter of prawns in Brazil. Check out the beach *barracas* for snacks and fast food.

🍴 Chaplin, Av Pres Café Filho 27, Praia dos Artistas. Traditional seafood restaurant with sea views. Part of a leisure complex with a bar, English pub and a nightclub.

🍴 Doux France, R Otâvio Lamartine, Petrópolis. Authentic French cuisine, outdoor seating.

🍴 Estação Trem de Minas, Av Pres Café Filho 197, Praia dos Artistas, T084-3202 2099. Charming rustic style, distinctly upmarket. 40 brands of *cachaça*, live music nightly, terrace and cocktails. Self-service lunch and dinner.

🍴 Raro Sabor, R Seridó 722, Petrópolis, T084-3202 1857. Exclusive bistro with Russian caviar on the menu.

🍴 A Macrobiótica, Princesa Isabel 524, Centro. Vegetarian restaurant and shop. Lunch only.

🍴 Bob's, Av Sen Salgado Filho. Daily 1000-2200. Hamburger chain.

🍴 Camarões Express, Av Sen Salgado Filho, Centro. Open for lunch only at weekends. Express prawns in 15 styles.

🍴 Carne de Sol Benigna Lira, R Dr José Augusto Bezerra de Medeiros 09, Praia do Meio. Traditional setting, regional cuisine.

🍴 Fiorentina, Augusto Bezerra de Medeiros 529, delivery T084-3202 0020. An Italian pizzeria with a huge range of seafood, try the lobster with spaghetti. Friendly service.

🍴 Peixada da Comadre, R Dr José Augusto Bezerra de Medeiros 4, Praia dos Artistas. Lively seafood restaurant with popular prawn dishes.

🍴 Saint Antoine, R Santo Antônio 651,

Cidade Alta, Centro. Mediocre self-service pay by weight establishment.

🍴-🍴 Farol Bar, Av Sílvio Pedrosa 105 (at the end of Via Costeira on Praia Areia Preta). Famous dried meat dishes – a local speciality.

Ponta Negra *p80, map p80*

🍴 Manary, Manary Praia Hotel, R Francisco Gurgel (see page 84). The best seafood in the city in a poolside restaurant overlooking Ponta Negra beach.

🍴 Roschti, Av Erivan França, T084-3219 4406. International cuisine in a relaxed beachfront bistro and more formal upstairs dining room.

🍴 Sobre Ondas, Av Erivan França 14, T084-3219 4222. Average seafood and international dishes in an intimate beach-front setting with an underwater theme.

🍴 Atlântico, Av Erivan França 27, T084-3219 2762. Relaxed, warm service, semi open-air, beachfront. Portuguese-owned, Italian and Portugese dishes, fish and *carne de sol*. Recommended.

🍴 Barraca do Caranguejo, Av Erivan França 1180, T084-3219 5069. Eight prawn dishes for US$8 and live music nightly from 2100.

🍴 Camarões, Av Eng Roberto Freire 2610. Also at Natal shopping centre. Touristy, but very good seafood.

🍴 Cipó Brasil, Av Erivan 3, T0800-3284051. Funky little Playa del Carmen-style bar with a jungle theme, 4 levels, sand floors, lantern-lit, very atmospheric. Average food (pizzas, crêpes), good cocktails, live music from 2100.

🍴 Ponta Negra Grill, Av Erivan 20, T084-3219 3714. A large, popular restaurant with live music and several terraces overlooking the beach. Steaks, seafood and cocktails.

🍴 Ponta Negra Mall. Stalls sell sandwiches and snacks.

Tibau do Sul and Pipa *p82*

There are many restaurants and bars along Pipa's main street, Av Baía dos Golfinhos.

ŸŸŸ Al Buchetto, Av Baía dos Golfinhos 837, Pipa, T084-3246 2318. Decent, Italian- made pasta and a lively atmosphere.

ŸŸŸ Camamo Beijupirá, Tibau do Sul, T084-3246 4195. One of the best restaurants in Brazil with a eclectic mix of fusion dishes like prawns and slices of leek in a spicy cashew sauce with raisins and ginger, served with fervent enthusiasm by owner Tadeu Lubambo. Excellent wine list.

ŸŸŸ Toca da Coruja, Praia da Pipa (see page 85). Superlative and beautifully presented regional food in a tropical garden setting. Intimate and romantic. Highly recommended.

ŸŸŸ Vivendo, Av Baía dos Golfinhos, Pipa. One of the town's best seafood restaurants and a good place to watch the passers-by.

Ÿ Casa de Taipe and Shirley-My House, Av Baía dos Golfinhos 1126 and 1213, Praia da Pipa. Very cheap but decent self-service restaurants, the latter owned by the sister of Vera of **Vera-My House** (see page 86).

Ÿ São Sebastião, R do Ceu, Pipa. Vegetarian and wholefood. Good value. Good juices.

Ÿ Sopa de Patrick/Chez Lisa, Av Baía dos Golfinhos s/n, Praia da Pipa. Generous portions of various delicious soups, in a little shack beyond the main square.

Ÿ Tatoo Batata, R do Ceu, Pipa, T084-9419 7181. Enormous baked potatoes with fillings likee cheese and sweet corn. Salads and juices too. Friendly owner. Next to **A Conchego** *pousada* (see Sleeping).

♪ Bars and clubs

Natal and around *p78, map p79*
Dance is an important pastime in Natal. In an area in the centre known as **Ribeira**, there are a few popular bars/nightclubs in restored historic buildings in R Chile.

Amiça, Av Engenheiro Roberto Freire s/n. New club with techno and house, popular with locals and tourists.

Blackout B52, R Chile 25, T084-3221 1282. Lively venue with a 1940s theme. The best night is 'Black Monday'. There is live rock,

blues and MPB on other nights. The crowd is 20s and early 30s.

Budda Pub, Av Engenheiro Roberto Freire (an annexe of the Tiberius). A little bar with good bar food and a laid-back atmosphere.

Centro de Turismo (see Shopping, below) has *Forró com Turista*, a chance for visitors to learn this fun dance, Thu at 2200. There are many other enjoyable venues where visitors are encouraged to join in.

Chaplin, Av Presidente Café Filho 27, Praia dos Artistas, T084-3202 1188. Different zones with everything from MPB and *forró* to techno and progressive house.

Novakapital, Av Presidente Café Filho 872, Praia dos Artistas, T084-3202 7111. With *forró*, live music, especially rock and foam parties, US$4, from 2400.

Ponta Negra *p80, map p80*
Although there is a handful of respectable clubs, Ponta Negra beach is now somewhat seedy. The municipal authorities are coming down very hard on the sex industry and its clients, and are installing video cameras all along the beach. Alto Ponta Negra is very lively and has live music and a range of bars and clubs open until dawn.

Baraonda, Av Erivan França 44, T084-9481 3748. Live music nightly except Tue, including *forró* and MPB from 2300 until late.

Taverna Pub, R Dr Manoel, Araújo 500, Alta Ponta Negra, T084-3236 3696. Medieval-style pub in youth hostel basement. Eclectic (rock, Brazilian pop, jazz, etc) live music Tue-Sun from 2200, best night Wed. Recommended.

In front of the Taverna is a cluster of small venues including **Tapiocaria Salsa Bar** and the **Calderão da Bruxa**.

Tibau do Sul and around *p82*
Tibau do Sul has various beach *barracas*. There is always something going on in Pipa, whatever the night and whatever the month.

Aruman, Av Baía dos Golfinhos, Pipa. Good cocktails and a trendy crowd.

Blue Bar, Av Baía dos Golfinhos, Pipa. Live *pagodé* and samba on Wed.

Calangos, Baía dos Golfinhos s/n (at the southern end of Pipa). A club with famous DJs like Patife. Techno and MPB Thu-Sun.

Carvalho do Fogo, Tibau do Sul. *Forró* until dawn every Wed.

Reggae Bar, just off Av Baía dos Golfinhos, Pipa centre. Live reggae bands, usually on Tue.

Festivals and events

Natal and around *p78, map p79*

Jan Festa de Nossa Senhora dos **Navegantes**, when numerous vessels go to sea from Praia da Redinha, north of town.

Mid-Oct Country show, **Festa do Boi** (bus marked Parnamirim to the exhibition centre), gives a good insight into rural life.

Mid-Dec Carnaval, the Salvador-style out-of-season carnival, a lively 4-day music festival with dancing in the streets.

Shopping

Natal and around *p78, map p79*

Centro de Turismo, R Aderbal de Figueiredo, 980, off R Gen Cordeiro, Petrópolis, T084-3212 2267. Sun-Wed 0900-1900, Thu 2200. A converted prison with a wide variety of handicraft and antiques shops, art gallery and tourist information booth. Good view of the Rio Potengi and the sea.

Centro Municipal de Artesanato, Av Pres Café Filho, Praia dos Artistas. Daily 1000-2200. Sand-in-bottle pictures are very common in Natal and there are plenty here alongside other touristy items.

Natal Shopping, Av Senador Salgado Filho, 2234, between Via Costeira and Ponta Negra. Large mall with restaurants, cinemas and 140 shops. Free shuttle service to major hotels.

Tibau do Sul and around *p82*

Pipa is a good place for raw cotton and costume jewellery made from tropical seeds.

The Bookshop (next to the **Reggae Bar**, see

Bars and clubs, above). Run by the wonderfully knowledgeable and eccentric Cyntia, who rents out books of all genres from Oscar Wilde to Dostoyevsky.

▲ Activities and tours

Natal and around *p78, map p79*
Boat trips

Boat trips on the Rio Potengi and along the nearby beaches of the Litoral Sul. A 2-hr tour includes hotel pickup, a snack, and allows time for a swim, US$25 per person. Boat trips to Barra do Cunhaú, 86 km south of Natal, go through mangroves, visit an island and a salt mine (Passeio Ecológico Cunhaú).

Buggy tours

Buggy tours are by far the most popular, US$40-90 and can be organized through the hotels. Be sure to check that only shifting dunes are visited. Fixed dunes are protected by Brazilian environmental law. It is possible to hire a buggy, or take a tour, all the way to Fortaleza (US$800 for 4 people) with companies like **Buggy e Compania**, www.buggyecia.com.br. Avoid the huge operators like **Brésil-Aventure** who journey in huge convoys. **Cariri Ecotours**, below, can recommend environmentally sensitive operators.

Dromedary rides

Cleide Gomes and Philippe Landry of **Dromedunas**, www.dromedunas.com.br, offer dromedary rides on the dunes above Genipabu. Walks last around 30 mins and they make a far more peaceful alternative to buzzing dune buggies. You'll find them on Genipabu beach from 0900 every day.

Ecotourism

Cariri Ecotours, R Francisco Gurgel 9067, Ponta Negra, T/F084-9928 0198, www.cariri ecotours.com.br. Excellent tours to some of the most interesting sights in the north-eastern interior, such as Souza, Cariri and the Serra da Capivara. Short on information about local fauna but good on history and geology.

Tibau do Sul and Pipa *p82*
Buggy tours to Barra de Cunhaú US$50, from Pipa to Natal US$115.

Genipabu *p83*
Associação dos Bugueiros,
T084-3225 2077. US$25 for dune buggy tour. Microlight flights are also available.

⊖ Transport

Natal and around *p78, map p79*
Air Buses to the airport run every 30 mins from the old *rodoviária* and are marked 'Aeroporto'. A taxi to the airport costs US$25; US$20 from Ponta Negra. There are flights to **Brasília, Fortaleza, Recife, Rio de Janeiro, Salvador, São Paulo; Belo Horizonte, Goiânia, São Luís, Fernando de Noronha, Vitória, Porto Alegre**. There are international flights to **Lisbon** with TAP.

Airline offices GOL, www.voe gol.com.br, at airport. **Oceanair**, www.Avianca.com.br. **TAM**, Av Campos Sales 500, Tirol, T084-3201 2020, at airport, T084-3643 1624, freephone T0800-123100, www.tam.com.br. **TAP**, www.flytap.com, has connections with Portugal. **TRIP**, T084-3234 1717, freephone T0800-2747, www.voetrip.com.br. **Varig**, R Mossoró 598, Centro, T084-3201 9339, at airport, T084-3743 1100, freephone T0800-997000, www.varig.com.br. **Webjet**, www.webjet.com.br.

Bus
Local Regional tickets are sold on street level of the new *rodoviária* in Cidade da Esperança; interstate tickets are available on the 2nd floor. A taxi to the bus station costs around US$25 from town, or US$18 from Ponta Negra, or there are regular local buses (see Ins and outs, page 78).

From the old *rodoviária* **Viação Campos** runs to **Pirangi**, US$0.60, 5 times a day 0630-1815, 3 on Sun 0730, 0930, 1645. In

summer, buses run from both *rodoviárias*, every 30 mins to **Pirangi**, US$2, 1 hr; to **Tabatinga** US$3, 1¼ hrs.

Long-distance From the new *rodoviária*, there are 6 buses a day to **Tibau do Sul**, US$5, 2 hrs, starting at 0600, and going on from Tibau to **Pipa**, US$7, 15 mins more.To **Recife** with Napoles, 5 daily, US$15 *convencional*, US$12 *executivo*, 4 hrs. With Nordeste to **Mossoró**, US$10 *convencional*, US$15 *executivo*, 4 hrs. To **Aracati**, US$14, 5½ hrs. To **Fortaleza**, US$15 *convencional*, US$210 *executivo*, US$35 *leito*, 8 hrs. To **João Pessoa**, every 2 hrs, US$4 *convencional*, US$8 *executivo*, 3 hrs. With São Geraldo to **Maceió**, buses both direct and via Recife, US$21 *convencional*, US$30 *executivo*, 10 hrs. To **Salvador**, US$50 *executivo*, 20 hrs. To **Rio de Janeiro**, US$90. To **São Paulo**, US$90 *convencional*, US$100*executivo*, 46-49 hrs. With Boa Esperança to **Teresina**, US$40 *convencional*, US$45 *executivo*, 17-20 hrs. To **Belém**, US$70, 32 hrs.

Car hire Car hire offices can be found at the airport and through mid- to top-range hotels. **Avis**, at airport, www.avis.com. **Hertz**, airport, www.hertz.com. **Localiza**, Av Nascimento de Castro 1792, www.localiza.com.

Tibau do Sul and Pipa *p82*
Bicycle hire From Blue Planet, Pipa. US$5 for a half day, US$10 full day.

Buggy It is possible to travel all the way to **Fortaleza** by buggy with **Top Buggy**, www.topbuggy.com.br, via the stunning Rio Grande do Norte dunes and beaches.

Bus *Combis* connect Pipa and Tibau until around 2300. 6 buses a day to **Natal**'s new *rodoviária*, US$5, 2 hrs, from Pipa via Tibau do Sul, leaving Pipa 0500-1600. Minivans also do this run and are easiest to catch from the beach.

Buses to **Paraíba** pass through Goianinha on

the interstate road. Frequent *combis* connect **Goianinha** with Pipa (30 mins, US$1.50).

Taxi Carlos, T084-9977 0006, after-hours taxi, speaks basic English.

Redinha *p83*
Bus Regular bus service from the old *rodoviária* to **Genipabu**.

Ferry There is a frequent ferry service to Cais Tavares de Lira, **Ribeira**, weekdays 0530-1900, weekend and holidays 0800-1830, US$1 per person, US$5 for car.

O Directory

Natal and around *p78, map p79*
Banks There are **Bradesco** and **HSBC** banks for international ATMs at the *rodoviária*, airport and throughout the city: **Banco 24 horas**, Natal Shopping, Cirrus, Visa, MasterCard and Plus. Also, Av Rio Branco 510, Cidade Alta, US$ cash and TCs at poor rates, cash advances against Visa, Mon-Fri 1000-1600. **Banespa**, Av Rio Branco 704, Cidade Alta, US$ cash and TCs at **dolar turismo** rate, Mon-Fri 1000-1430. **Sunset Câmbio**, Av Hermes da Fonseca 628, Tirol, T084-3212 2552, cash and TCs, 0900-1700. **Dunas Câmbio**, Av Roberto Freire 1776, Loja B-11, Capim Macio (east of Parque das Dunas), T084-3219 3840, cash and TCs, 0900-1700. **Embassies and consulates Germany**, R Gov Sílvio Pedrosa 308, Areia Preta, T084-3222 3596. **Italy**, R Auta de Souza 275, Centro, T084-3222 6674. **Spain**, R Amintas Barros 4200, Lagoa Nova, T084-206 5610. **Internet** Internet cafés on Ponta Negra and around the main beach areas. **Post office** R Princesa Isabel 711, Centro; Av Rio Branco 538, Centro; Av Engenheiro Hildegrando de Góis 22, Ribeira. **Poste restante** is in Ribeira, near the old *rodoviária*, at Av Rio Branco and Av General Gustavo Cordeiro de Farias, hard to find. **Police** Tourist police (Delegacia do Turista): T084-3236 3288, 24 hrs. **Telephone** R Princesa Isabel 687 and R João Pessoa, Centro, also a the *rodoviária*.

Ponta Negra *p80, map p80*
Banks Banco do Brasil, Seafront ATM for Cirrus, Visa, MasterCard and Plus. **Embassies and consulates Canada**, Av Roberto Freire 2951, bloco 01, loja 09-CCAB Sul, T084-3219 2197. **Internet Sobre Ondas** (also bar and restaurant, see Eating), 0900-2400, 10 centavos 1 min. **Post office** Av Praia de Ponta Negra 8920. **Telephone** Av Roberto Freire 3100, Shopping Cidade Jardim, Av Roberto Freire.

Ceará

Ceará calls itself the 'Terra da Luz' (Land of Light) and much of its 573-km coastline and bone-dry interior is baked under permanent sunshine. It could just as well be called the land of wind: kitesurfers and windsurfers are quickly discovering that there is nowhere better in the world for their sports. Locations such as Cumbuco and Jericoacoara are blown by strong winds almost 365 days a year, and the Atlantic Ocean offers varied conditions from glassy flat through to rolling surf. Ceará boasts some beautiful beaches, too – though poor when compared to the rest of Brazil perhaps – with long, broad stretches of sand backed by ochre cliffs or towering dunes. Sadly they are increasingly populated by expat and profiteering foreigners. Many of the little fishing villages that lay undiscovered for decades are losing their character to ugly condos and concrete hotels. In places like Canoa Quebrada, Jericoacoara and Cumbuco, other European languages are spoken as much as Portuguese. Even the state capital Fortaleza has been affected. Plane-loads of foreign tourists have turned its once-lively nightlife increasingly tawdry; and while the state authorities are cracking down hard on the exploitation locals in the main tourist towns are often cynical about foreigners.

» *For listings, see pages 108-121.*

Fortaleza → *For listings, see pages 108-121. Phone code: 085. Population: 2.1 million.*

Brazil's fifth largest city is a stretch of concrete towers along a series of white-sand beaches behind a gloriously misty green and blue Atlantic dotted with rusting wrecks. The water temperature is permanently in the high 20s and there's a constant sea breeze. The sea is surprisingly clean, even in Iracema near the centre, but the best beaches for swimming are further east and west.

Fortaleza has a long history and a number if sights of historic interest. However, most tourists are drawn here by the city's reputation for lively nightlife. The sound of *forró* still reverberates in the streets behind Iracema beach, but nowadays it's hard to find anywhere that isn't overrun with groups of single foreign men and professional local women. Many locals are angry about their city's poor reputation and are wary of tourists. There are signs that this is changing, however – police and local hotel owners have been making concerted efforts to discourage the growth of this kind of tourism and are coming down increasingly hard on any locals and foreigners involved.

Ins and outs

Getting there International and domestic flights arrive at **Aeroporto Pinto Martins** ① *Praça Eduardo Gomes, 6 km south of the centre, T085-3392 1200*. There are connections with São Luís and Belém, as well as the Guianas, various destinations in Portugal and Italy. The airport has a 24-hour tourist office, T085-3477 1667, car hire, a food hall, internet facilities, bookstore, **Banco do Brasil** for exchange and **Bradesco** and **HSBC** for international ATMs. Bus No 404 runs from the airport to Praça José de Alencar in the centre, US$1.50. **Expresso Guanabara** minibuses run to the *rodoviária* and Beira Mar (US$2). Bus No 066 runs from Papicu to Parangaba; bus No 027 runs from Papicu to Siqueira. Taxis to the centre, Avenida Beira Mar or Praia do Futuro charge a fixed fee of US$25, or US$30 at night (30 minutes, allowing for traffic).

Interstate buses arrive at the **Rodoviária São Tomé** ① *Av Borges de Melo 1630, Fátima, 6 km south of the centre, T085-3256 2100*. Information is available from *Disque Turismo* booth, open 0600-1800, which also has lockers for storing luggage.

Opposite the *rodoviária* is **Hotel Amuarama**, which has a bar and restaurant; there's also a *lanchonete*. Many city buses run to the centre (US$1) including No 78, which goes to Iracema via the Centro Dragão do Mar. If in doubt, the tourist information booth will point you in the right direction. A taxi to Praia de Iracema, or Avenida Abolição costs around US$15. Minivans to Jericoacoara leave from in front of the Hotel **Casa Blanca** (see Sleeping, page 108). ►► *See Transport, page 118.*

Getting around The city is spread out, with its main attractions in the centre and along the seashore; transport from one to the other can take a long time. The city bus system is efficient if a little rough; buses and vans cost US$1 per journey. The cheapest way to orientate yourself within the city is to take the 'Circular 1' (anti-clockwise) or 'Circular 2' (clockwise) buses which pass Avenida Beira Mar, the Aldeota district, the university (UFC) and cathedral via Meireles, Iracema, Centro Dragão do Mar and the Centre, US$1.50. Alternatively, take the new *Top Bus* run by **Expresso Guanabara** ① *T0800-991992, US$2.50*, an air-conditioned minibus starting at Avenida Abolição.

When driving outside the city, have a good map and be prepared to ask directions frequently as road signs are non-existent or are placed after junctions.

Tourist information The main office of the state tourism agency, Setur ① *Secretária do Turismo do Estado do Ceará, Av General Afonso Albuquerque Lima, Fortaleza T085-3101 4688, www.setur.ce.gov.br*, has maps and brochures and can help with hotels and tours. There are also information booths at the airport and *rodoviária*, and at the Farol de Mucuripe (old lighthouse), open 0700-1730. The **Posta Telefônica Beira Mar** ① *Av Beira Mar, almost opposite Praiano Palace Hotel*, provides information, sells *combi* tickets to Jericoacoara, and has postcards, clothes and magazines. If you have problems, contact the **tourist police** ① *R Silva Paulet 505, Aldeota, T085-3433 8171*.

Safety The city is generally safe for visitors. However, tourists should avoid the following areas: Serviluz favela between the old lighthouse (Avenida Vicente de Castro), Mucuripe

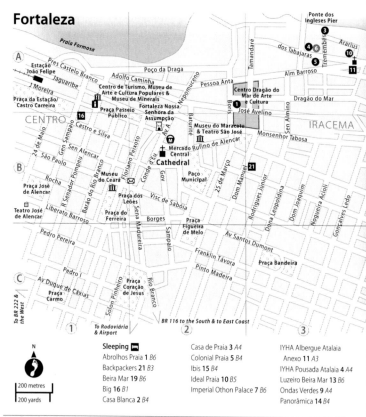

Fortaleza

Sleeping 🛏
Abrolhos Praia **1** *B6*
Backpackers **21** *B3*
Beira Mar **19** *B6*
Big **16** *B1*
Casa Blanca **2** *B4*

Casa de Praia **3** *A4*
Colonial Praia **5** *B4*
Ibis **15** *B4*
Ideal Praia **10** *B5*
Imperial Othon Palace **7** *B4*

IYHA Albergue Atalaia
  Anexo **11** *A3*
IYHA Pousada Atalaia **4** *A4*
Luzeiro Beira Mar **13** *B6*
Ondas Verdes **9** *A4*
Panorâmica **14** *B4*

and Praia do Futuro; the favela behind the railway station; the Passeio Público at night; and Avenida Abolição at its eastern (Nossa Senhora da Saúde church) and western ends.

Sights

Walking through the centre of Fortaleza, it is hard to ignore the city's history, which dates back to the 17th century. Pedestrian walkways radiate from the **Praça do Ferreira**, the heart of the commercial centre, and the whole area is dotted with shady green squares. The **Fortaleza Nossa Senhora da Assumpção** ① *Av Alberto Nepomuceno, T085-3255 1600, telephone in advance for permission to visit, daily 0800-1100, 1400-1700*, originally built in 1649 by the Dutch, gave the city its name. Near the fort, on Rua Dr João Moreira, is the 19th-century **Praça Passeio Público** (or Praça dos Mártires), a park with old trees and statues of Greek deities. West of here a neoclassical former prison (1866) houses a fine tourist centre, the **Centro de Turismo do Estado (Emcetur)** ① *Av Senador Pompeu 350, near the waterfront, T0800-991516, closed Sun*, with museums, theatre and craft shops. It houses the renovated **Museu de Arte e Cultura Populares** and the **Museu de Minerais**

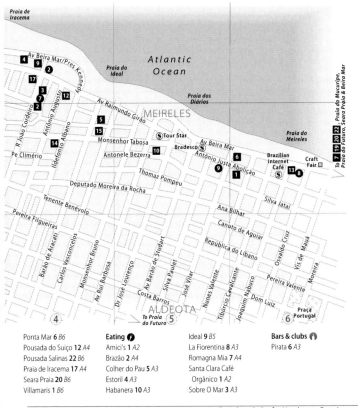

Ponta Mar **6** *B6*	**Eating** 🍴	Ideal **9** *B5*	**Bars & clubs** 🍸
Pousada do Suíço **12** *A4*	Amici's **1** *A2*	La Fiorentina **8** *A3*	Pirata **6** *A3*
Pousada Salinas **22** *B6*	Brazão **2** *A4*	Romagna Mia **7** *A4*	
Praia de Iracema **17** *A4*	Colher do Pau **5** *A3*	Santa Clara Café	
Seara Praia **20** *B6*	Estoril **4** *A3*	Orgânico **1** *A2*	
Villamaris **1** *B6*	Habanera **10** *A3*	Sobre O Mar **3** *A3*	

① *T085-3212 3566*. Further west along Rua Dr João Moreira, at **Praça Castro Carreira** (commonly known as Praça da Estação), is the nicely refurbished train station, **Estação João Felipe** (1880), which runs commuter services.

The **Teatro José de Alencar** ① *Praça José de Alencar, T085-3229 1989, Mon-Fri 0800-1700, hourly tours, some English-speaking guides, US$1, Wed free*, was inaugurated in 1910 and is worth a visit. It is a magnificent iron structure imported from Scotland and decorated in neoclassical and art nouveau styles. It also houses a library and art gallery. The **Praça dos Leões** or Praça General Tibúrcio on Rua Conde D'Eu has bronze lions imported from France. Around it stand the 18th-century **Palácio da Luz** ① *T085-3231 5699*, former seat of the state government, and the **Igreja Nossa Senhora do Rosário**, built by slaves in the 18th century. Also here is the former provincial legislature, dating from 1871, which houses the **Museu do Ceará** ① *R São Paulo, next to Praça dos Leões, T085-3251 1502, Tue-Fri 0830-1730, Sat 0830- 1400, US$0.80*. The museum has displays on history and anthropology. To get there, take bus marked 'Dom Luís'.

The new **cathedral** ① *Praça da Sé*, completed in 1978, in Gothic style but constructed out of concrete with beautiful stained-glass windows, stands beside the new semi-circular **Mercado Central**.

There are several worthwhile museums to visit in and around Fortaleza. The **Museu do Maracatu** ① *Rufino de Alencar 231*, at Teatro São José, has costumes of this ritual dance of African origin. The new and exciting **Centro Dragão do Mar de Arte e Cultura** ① *R Dragão do Mar 81, Praia de Iracema, T085-3488 8600, www.dragaodomar.org.br, Tue-Thu 1000- 1730, Fri-Sun 1400-2130, US$0.75 for entry to each museum/gallery, free on Sun*, hosts concerts, dance performances and exhibitions of art and photography. It has various entrances, from Rua Almirante Barroso, Rua Boris, and from the junction of Monsenhor Tabosa, Dom Manuel and Castelo Branco. The latter leads directly to three museums: on street level, the **Memorial da Cultura Cearense**, with changing exhibitions; on the next floor down is an art and cultural exhibition; in the basement is an excellent audio-visual museum of **El Vaqueiro**. Also at street level is the **Livraria Livro Técnico**. There is a **planetarium** with a whispering gallery underneath. The centre also houses the **Museu de Arte Contemporânea do Ceará**. This area is very lively at night.

Some 15 km south of the centre, the **Museu Artur Ramos** ① *in the Casa de José de Alencar, Av Perimetral, Messejana, T085-3229 1898, Mon 1400-1730, Tue-Sun 0800-1200, 1400-1700*, displays artefacts of African and indigenous origin collected by the anthropologist Artur Ramos, as well as documents from the writer José de Alencar.

Beaches

The urban beaches between Barra do Ceará (west) and Ponta do Mucuripe (east) are polluted and not suitable for swimming. Minibus day tours for other beaches, from US$6, and transfers to Jericoacoara, US$15, leave from along the seafront. The agency **CPVTUR** ① *Av Monsenhor Tabosa 1001, T085-3219 2511*, also runs trips.

Heading east from the centre, **Praia de Iracema** is one of the older beach suburbs, with some original early 20th-century houses. It is not much of a sunbathing beach as it has little shade or facilities and swimming is unsafe, but at night it is very lively. Of its many bars and restaurants, the **Estoril**, housed in one of the earliest buildings, has become a landmark. The Ponte Metálica or **Ponte dos Ingleses**, nearby, was built by the British Civil engineering firm, Norton Griffiths and Company, in 1921 as a commercial jetty for the port, but was never completed due to lack of funds, and re-opened as a promenade pier in imitation of English seaside piers. It was and is now a very popular spot for watching the sunset and the occasional pod of visiting dolphins.

East of Iracema, the **Avenida Beira Mar** (Avenida Presidente Kennedy) connects **Praia do Meireles** (divided into **Praia do Ideal**, **Praia dos Diários** and Praia do Meireles itself) with Volta da Jurema and Praia do Mucuripe; it is lined with high-rise buildings and most luxury hotels are located here. A *calçado* (walkway), following the palm-lined shore, becomes a night-time playground as locals promenade on foot, roller skates, skateboards and bicycles. Children ride mini-motorbikes, scooters or the 'happiness' train with its Disney characters. Take in the spectacle while sipping an *agua de coco* or *caiprinha* on the beachfront, where there are volleyball courts, bars, open-air shows and a crafts fair in front of the Imperial Othon Palace Hotel.

Praia do Mucuripe, 5 km east of the centre, is Fortaleza's main fishing centre, where *jangadas* (traditional rafts with triangular sails) bring in the catch; there are many restaurants serving *peixada* and other fish specialities. The symbol of this beach is the statue of Iracema, the main character of the romance by José de Alencar. From the monument there is a good view of Mucuripe's port and bay. At Mucuripe Point is a **lighthouse** built by slaves in 1846, which houses the **Museu de Fortaleza** (now sadly run down and not a safe area, according to the tourist office). There is a lookout at the new lighthouse, good for viewing the *jangadas*, which return in the late afternoon, and the sunset.

Praia do Futuro, 8 km southeast of the centre, is the most popular bathing beach. It is 8 km long with strong waves, sand dunes and freshwater showers, but no natural shade. Vendors in straw shacks serve local dishes such as crab. On Thursday nights it becomes the centre for the city's nightlife, with people enjoying live music and *forró*. The south end of the beach is known as **Caça e Pesca**; water here is polluted because of the outflow of the Rio Cocó. Praia do Futuro has few hotels or buildings because the salt-spray corrosion is among the strongest in the world.

At **Praia de Sabiaguaba**, 20 km southeast of the centre, is a small fishing village known for its seafood; the area has mangroves and is good for fishing.

Some 29 km southeast of the centre is **Praia Porto das Dunas**, a pleasant beach that is popular for watersports, such as surfing. Buggies and microlight tours can be arranged. The main attraction is **Beach Park** ① *US$20,* the largest water park in South America, with pools, water toboggans, sports fields and restaurants.

The coast east of Fortaleza → *For listings, see pages 108-121.*

The most prominent feature of the eastern coast is the impressive coloured sand cliffs. There are also freshwater springs near the shore, along with palm groves and mangroves. Lobster fishing is one of the main activities. It is possible to hike along much of the eastern coast: from Prainha to Águas Belas takes seven hours (bring plenty of water and sun protection). Where there are rivers to cross, there is usually a boatmen. Fishing villages have accommodation or hammock space.

Ins and outs There are regular buses to the beaches and to the city of Aquiraz from the *rodoviária* in Fortaleza. For further information on the area, including accommodation and restaurants, visit www.aquiraz.ce.gov.br.

Aquiraz and around → *Phone code: 085. Population: 61,000.*

Some 31 km east of Fortaleza, Aquiraz was the original capital of Ceará. It retains several colonial buildings and has a religious art museum. It is also the access point for a number of beaches.

Six kilometres east of Aquiraz, **Prainha** is a fishing village and weekend resort with a 10-km beach and dunes. The beach is clean and largely empty and the waves are good for surfing. You can see *jangadas* coming in daily in the late afternoon. The village is known for its lacework; the women using the *bilro* and *labirinto* techniques at the **Centro de Rendeiras**. In some of the small restaurants it is possible to see displays of the *carimbó*, one of the north Brazilian dances. Just south of Prainha is **Praia do Presídio**, with gentle surf, dunes, palms and *cajueiros* (cashew trees).

About 18 km southeast of Aquiraz is **Praia Iguape**, another fishing village known for its lacework. The beach is a large, elbow-shaped sandbank, very scenic especially at Ponta do Iguape. Nearby are high sand dunes where sand-skiing is popular. There is a lookout at Morro do Enxerga Tudo; one-hour *jangada* trips cost US$8.50. Lacework is sold at the **Centro de Rendeiras**. Locals are descendants of Dutch, Portuguese and indigenous peoples; some traditions such as the *coco-de-praia* folk dance are still practised. Some 3 km south of Iguape is **Praia Barro Preto**, a wide tranquil beach, with dunes, palms and lagoons.

Cascavel → *Phone code: 085.*

Cascavel, 62 km southeast of Fortaleza, has a Saturday crafts fair by the market. It is the access point for the beaches of Caponga and Águas Belas, where traditional fishing villages coexist with fancy weekend homes and hotels. **Caponga**, 15 km northeast of Cascavel, has a wide, 2-km-long beach lined with palms. *Jangadas* set sail in the early morning; arrangements can be made to accompany fishermen on overnight trips, a 90-minute ride costs US$14 for up to five people. There is a fish market and crafts sales (ceramics, embroidery and lacework) on the beach. A 30-minute walk south along the white-sand beach leads to **Águas Belas**, at the mouth of the Rio Mal Cozinhado, offering a combination of fresh and saltwater bathing (access also by road, 15 km from Cascavel, 4 km from Caponga). The scenery here, and 5 km further east at Barra Nova, changes with the tide. A walk north along the beach for 6 km takes you to the undeveloped **Praia do Batoque**, which is surrounded by cliffs and dunes.

Morro Branco and Praia das Fontes → *Phone code: 085.*

Beberibe, 78 km from Fortaleza, is the access point for Morro Branco and Praia das Fontes, some of the better-known beaches of the east coast.

About 4 km from Beberibe, **Morro Branco** has a spectacular beach, coloured craggy cliffs and beautiful views. *Jangadas* leave the beach at 0500, returning at 1400-1500. Lobster is the main catch in this area. The coloured sands of the dunes are bottled into beautiful designs and sold along with other crafts such as lacework, embroidery and straw goods. *Jangadas* may be hired for sailing (one hour for up to six people US$30). Beach buggies cost US$100 for a full day; taxis are also available for hire. The beach is lined with summer homes and can get very crowded during peak season.

South of Morro Branco and 6 km from Beberibe is **Praia das Fontes**, which also has coloured cliffs with freshwater springs. There is a fishing village and, at the south end, a lagoon. Near the shore is a cave, known as **Mãe de Água**, visible at low tide. Buggies and microlights can be hired on the beach. A luxury resort complex has been built here, making the area expensive.

South of Praia das Fontes are several less developed beaches including **Praia Uruaú** or **Marambaia**, about 6 km from Praia das Fontes along the beach or 21 km by road from Beberibe, via Sucatinga on a sand road. The beach is at the base of coloured dunes; there is a fishing village with some accommodation. Just inland is **Lagoa do Uruaú**, the largest in the state and a popular place for watersports. A buggy from Morro Branco costs US$45 for four people.

About 50 km southeast of Beberibe is **Fortim**. From here, boats run to **Pontal de Maceió**, a reddish sand point at the mouth of the Rio Jaguaribe, from where there is a good view of the eastern coast. In the winter the river is high and there is fishing for shrimp; in the summer it dries up, forming islands and freshwater beaches. There's a fishing village about 1 km from the ocean with bars, restaurants and small *pousadas*.

Prainha do Canto Verde → *Phone code: 085.*

Some 120 km east of Fortaleza, in the district of Beberibe, is Prainha do Canto Verde, a small fishing village on a vast beach, which has an award-winning community tourism project. There are guesthouses or houses for rent (see Sleeping, page 110), restaurants (good food at **Sol e Mar**) and a handicraft cooperative. Each November there is a **Regata Ecológica**, with *jangadas* from up and down the coast competing. *Jangada* and catamaran cruises are offered, as well as fishing and a number of walking trails. This a simple place, where people make their living through artesanal fishing, without the use of big boats or industrial techniques. The village has built up its tourism infrastructure without any help from outside investors, and has been fighting the foreign speculators since 1979. The people are friendly and visitors are welcome to learn about the traditional way of life, although knowledge of Portuguese is essential.

Ins and outs To get to Prainha do Canto Verde, take a São Benedito bus to Aracati or Canoa Quebrada, buy a ticket to Quatro Bocas and ask to be let off at Lagoa da Poeira, two hours from Fortaleza. If you haven't booked a transfer in advance, Márcio at the **Pantanal** restaurant at the bus stop may be able to take you, US$2.75. The website www.fortal net.com.br/~fishnet, is a good source of information.

Aracati → *Phone code: 088. Population: 62,000.*

Situated on the shores of the Rio Jaguaribe, Aracati is the access point to the Ceará's most southeasterly beaches. The city is best known for its **Carnaval** (the liveliest in the state) and for its colonial architecture, including several 18th-century churches and mansions with Portuguese tile façades. There is a **religious art museum** (closed lunchtime and Sunday afternoon), a Saturday morning crafts fair on Avenida Coronel Alexandrino, and a number of simple *pousadas* (**$$-$**) on the same street.

Canoa Quebrada → *Phone code: 088.*

Canoa Quebrada stands on a sand dune 10 km from Aracati backed by crumbling, multi-coloured sandstone cliffs. It remained an isolated fishing village until 1982, when a road was built. It is now a very popular resort, with many package hotels, busy bars and restaurants. But the village is almost entirely devoid of its once legendary laid-back, weed smoking hippy beach feel. The nightlife is good in season (especially over Christmas, New Year and Carnaval, when it can be very difficult to find a room). Canoa is famous for its *labirinto* lacework, coloured sand sculpture and beaches. Sand skiing is popular on the dunes and there is good windsurfing and kitesurfing on the Jaguaribe estuary, just outside town, with plenty of options for lessons and equipment rental (see page 117).

Local fishermen have their homes in **Esteves**, a separate village also on top of the cliff; they still live off the sea and rides on *jangadas*, buggy tours and light adventure on zip lines and sandboards can easily be organized in town or on the beach.

Ins and outs Canoa is served by at least four daily buses from Fortaleza; *expresso* or *leito* are fastest. Very frequent *combi* vans connect to Arati from where there are connections into Rio Grande do Norte. Note that the nearest place to change money or find an international ATM is in Aracati. To avoid biting insects and *bicho do pé* (burrowing fleas that frequent dirty beaches), it is best to wear shoes or sandals. For more information, including extensive accommodation listings, visit www.portalcanoaquebrada.com.br.

South of Canoa Quebrada

Heading south from Canoa Quebrada, **Porto Canoa** is a resort town that opened in 1996, fashioned after the Greek islands. It includes beach homes and apartments, shopping areas, restaurants and hotels, and there are facilities for watersports, horse riding, microlight flights, buggy and *jangada* outings.

South of here, **Majorlândia** is a very pleasant village with multi-coloured sand dunes, used in bottle pictures and cord crafts, and a wide beach with strong waves that are good for surfing. The arrival of the fishing fleet in the evening is an important daily event; lobster is the main catch. It is a popular weekend destination with beach homes for rent and plenty of *pousadas*. Unlike many beach locations in Ceará, the area is predominantly Brazilian. **Carnaval** here is quite lively, but you will have no trouble finding a room outside the peak season. The town is easy to find your way around.

About 5 km south along the beach from Majorlândia is the village of **Quixaba**, on a beach surrounded by coloured cliffs, with reefs offshore and good fishing. At low tide you can reach the popular destination of **Lagoa do Mato**, some 4 km south. The *lagoa* can also be reached by buggy from Canoa Quebrada beach (US$30 for four people). There's a hotel, restaurant and pristine beach surrounded by dunes, cliffs and palms.

Ponta Grossa → *Phone code: 088.*

Ponta Grossa, 30 km southeast of Aracati near Icapuí, is the last municipality before Rio Grande do Norte (access from Mossoró) and is reached via a sand road just before Redonda. It's a very pretty place, nestled at the foot of the cliffs, with a beautiful beach.

Ponta Grossa has its own tourism development initiative. The fishing community has many members of Dutch origin, following a shipwreck in the 19th century, and many people have fair hair. It is also one of the few places where *peixe boi marinho* (manatees) can be spotted. There's a good lookout from the cliffs (four-hour buggy ride, US$75 for four).

Beach trips go from Canoa Quebrada (see above) to Ponta Grossa for lunch, but it is possible to stay here (it helps if you can speak Portuguese). A number of cabins are being built and there are several restaurants/bars. The tourism coordinator is Eliabe, T088-3432

5001/9964 5846. For information on community tourism and the preservation of traditional ways of life in Ceará, contact **Instituto Terramar** ① *R Pinho Pessoa 86, Joaquim Távora, Fortaleza, T085-3226 4154/8804 0999, ask for Esther Neuhaus, www.terramar.org.br.*

To the south are the beaches of **Redonda**, another very pretty place, and **Barreiras**, which is good for surfing and has a handful of hotels.

The coast west of Fortaleza → *For listings, see pages 108-121.*

The coast northwest of Fortaleza has many wide beaches backed by fixed or shifting dunes, and surrounded by swathes of coconut groves. The main roads are some distance from the shore, making access to the beaches more difficult than on the eastern coast. This means the fishing villages have retained a more traditional lifestyle and a responsible attitude towards travel is especially important.

Praia Barra do Ceará
This long beach lies 8 km northwest of the centre of Fortaleza, where the Rio Ceará flows into the sea (take a 'Grande Circular 1' bus). Here are the ruins of the 1603 **Forte de Nossa Senhora dos Prazeres**, the first Portuguese settlement in the area, partially covered by dunes, from which you can watch the beautiful sunsets. The palm-fringed beaches west of the Rio Ceará are cleaner but have strong waves. An iron bridge has been built across this river, making the area more accessible and open to development, as at **Praia de Icaraí**, 22 km to the northwest, and **Tabuba**, 5 km further north.

Cumbuco
Cumbuco is a long, white-sand beach backed by foreign-owned hotels and condominiums, a few palms and a handful of little beach shacks; and has a problem with rubbish. The beach itself is nothing special, unless you're a kitesurfer in which case you'll be amazed. There is no better place in Brazil and perhaps the world to learn how to kitesurf; ideal conditions can be guaranteed almost every day of the year. Sadly, as Cumbuco is largely European-owned and locals can no longer afford to buy property here, the town has entirely lost its Brazilian personality. Portuguese is rarely heard and the only locals that remain work in the hotels or restaurants. As well as kitesurfing and windsurfing, there are buggies, horse riding and *jangadas*, as well as dunes (known locally as *skibunda*), which you can slide down into the freshwater **Lagoa de Parnamirim**. A buggy tour costs around US$15 per person.

Cumbuco is served by regular buses from Fortaleza. Allow one to two hours for the journey. For more information visit www.kite-surf-brazil.com.

Pecém and Taíba → *Phone code: 085. Population: 5500 (Pecém).*
Some 58 km northwest of Fortaleza, **Pecém** is a village set in a cove with a wide beach, dunes and inland lagoons. There is strong surf and surfing and fishing championships are held here. From Pecém it is 19 km by road to **Taíba**, a 14-km-long beach with a long palm-covered point extending into the sea. Nearby is **Siupé**, a village that maintains colonial characteristics, where embroidered hammocks, a trademark of Ceará, are made.

Pecém and Taíba are serviced by regular buses from Fortaleza; both have a few simple *pousadas*. The town's central telephone exchange can be reached on T085-344 1064 and T085-3340 1328; any three-digit numbers listed are extensions on these central lines.

Paracuru and Lagoinha → *Phone code: 085. Population: 28,000 (Paracuru).*

Some 106 km northwest of Fortaleza, **Paracuru** is a fishing port which hosts the most important **Carnaval** on the northwest coast, including street dancing and parades, decorated boats, sports championships and a beauty contest. It has some lovely deserted white-sand beaches with good bathing and surfing, and the people are very friendly. There are several *pousadas* in the centre. Restaurant **Ronco do Mar** has good fish dishes. **Boca do Poço** bar has *forró* at weekends. Buses from Fortaleza run at least every hour during the day to the central *rodoviária*, US$5.

West of Paracuru and 12 km from the town of Paraipaba is **Lagoinha**, a very scenic beach with hills, dunes and palms by the shore. There's a fishing village on one of the hills and nearby are some small but pleasant waterfalls. About 3 km west of town is **Lagoa da Barra**, a lake surrounded by dunes. Local legend says that one of the hills, Morro do Cascudo, has hidden treasure left by French pirates. There are six daily buses from Fortaleza to Paracuru and frequent transfers from there to Lagoinha (Brasileiro, three hours, US$6); there are plenty of cheap seafood restaurants and *pousadas*.

Fleixeiras and around → *Phone code: 085.*

Further northwest, some 135 km from Fortaleza, is **Trairi**, access point to a series of beaches that have kept their natural beauty and, until the mid-1990s, were untouched by tourism. North of Trairi, 15 km by road, is **Fleixeiras**, where pools that are good for snorkelling form near the beach at low tide. There are three daily buses from Fortaleza to Fleixeiras (US$7, information T085-3272 4128).

About 5 km west is **Imboaca**, a scenic beach with interesting rock formations and shifting dunes. Further west, at the mouth of the Rio Mundaú, is **Mundaú**, another beautiful area, with a beach, palms, dunes and an old working lighthouse. Take a raft across to the spit and walk for hours on deserted sands, see wind-eroded dunes or take a boat from the quay up the river to see the mangroves. Access roads from Imboaca and Cana to the south are often impassable because of shifting dunes; at low tide it is possible to reach it along the beach from Fleixeiras. There is a fishing village near the beach with some *pousadas* and restaurants.

Jericoacoara → *For listings, see pages 108-121. Phone code: 088.*

Jericoacoara is another of the northeast's paradise beaches that is getting spoilt. Up until the 1980s it was a magical place: a collection of little fishermen's shacks lost under towering dunes and surrounded by wonderful long, sweeping beaches. São Paulo middle-class hippies used to live here for months, surfing, dancing *forró* and smoking copious amounts of weed. Slowly Jeri began to grow. Then buggies began to race up and down the dunes – including the most delicate, those with fixed vegetation – and local villages started to become tourist attractions. In the 1980s, the Italians discovered Jeri and building began, much of it with braggadocio and little or no environmental considerations; buggies whizzed up and down from dawn to dusk like a plague of motorized flies. Today, few properties or tourism businesses are locally owned and the fishermen and their families are being sidelined and priced out of town.

That said, Jeri remains beautiful and it has a long way to go before it becomes as spoilt as Morro de São Paulo, Canoa Quebrada or Cumbuco. If careful choices are made by tourists (such as supporting local businesses, trying to speak Portuguese, participating in Brazilian culture and avoiding buggy tours and large European-run beachfront resorts), it could turn itself into an inspiring sustainable, small-scale resort (see box, above). The nearby beaches offer superb conditions for kitesurfing and windsurfing – both practices that do little to damage the environment – and there is excellent walking and cycling along the long flat beaches to beauty spots like the crumbling chocolate-coloured rock arch at **Pedra Furada**. Sandboarding is popular and watching the sunset from the top of the large dune just west of town, followed by a display of *capoeira* on the beach, is a tradition among visitors.

Ins and outs

There are two direct buses a day from Fortaleza to Jijoca from where *jardineiras* (Toyota pickups) do the 45-minute transfer to Jeri. Be sure to take a *VIP* or *executivo* as the journey takes five to six hours (seven to eight hours on other buses). It is far more comfortable to take an air-conditioned mini-van; these can be organized through *pousadas* in Jeri. Hotels and tour operators run two- to three-day tours from from Fortaleza. If not on a tour, 'guides' will besiege new arrivals in Jijoca with offers of buggies, or guiding cars through the tracks and dunes to Jeri for US$8. If you don't want to do this, ask if a pickup is going or contact **Francisco Nascimento** ① *O Chicão, at Posta do Dê, or T088-3669 1356*, who charges US$5 per person for the 22-km journey (30 minutes). There are connections with the rest of the state through Sobral. Arrivals from Maranhão and Piauí come via Parnaíba (see page 109) and Camocim. There are no banks in town; most *pousadas* and restaurants accept Visa but it is wise to bring plenty of cash in reais. ▶▶ *See Transport, page 119.*

Around Jericoacoara

Going west along the beach takes you through a succession of sand dunes and coconut groves; the views are beautiful. After 2 km is the beach of **Mangue Seco**, and 2 km beyond this is an arm of the ocean that separates it from **Guriú** (across the bridge), where there is a village on top of a fixed dune. There is good birdwatching here and if you wish to stay hammock space can be found. The village musician sings his own songs in the bar. It's a four-hour walk from Jericoacoara, or take a boat across the bay.

The best surfing, kitesurfing and windsurfing is 10 minutes from town on the pebbly **Praia de Malhada**, reachable either by walking east along the beach or by cutting through town. Top-quality equipment can be rented in Jeri. A 3- to 4-km walk to the east takes you to the **Pedra Furada**, a stone arch sculpted by the sea, one of the landmarks of Jeri, only accessible at low tide (check the tide tables at the **Casa do Turismo**). Swimming is dangerous here as waves and currents are strong. In the same direction but just inland is **Serrote**, a large hill with a lighthouse on top; it is well worth walking up for the magnificent views.

The best kitesurfing and windsurfing beaches are beyond Jeri, some 15 km east of town (43 km by road via Jijoca and Caiçara), at **Praia do Preá** and **Praia de Guriú**. Both beaches are reachable on day tours for around US$50 if you have your own kitesurf. Tours including equipment (US$60) can be arranged in Jeri through www.kiteclubprea.com. There is accommodation on both beaches. At low tide on Preá, you can visit the **Pedra da Seréia**, a rock pocked with natural swimming pools.

Some of the best scenery in the area is around **Nova Tatajuba**, about 35 km west of Jerí. One Toyota a day passes through the town on the way to the ferry point at Camocim and almost all buggy tours visit. There are simple *pousadas* and restaurants and the village is far smaller and less touristy than Jeri. ♦♦ *See Sleeping, page 111.*

Some 10 km beyond Praia do Preá (62 km by road) is the beach of **Barrinha**, with access to the picturesque **Lagoa Azul**. From here it's 10 km inland through the dunes (20 km along the road) to **Lagoa Paraíso** or **Jijoca**, a turquoise, freshwater lake, great for bathing (buggy US$10 per person).

Cruz

Some 40 km east of Jijoca is Cruz, an obligatory stop if travelling by bus from Sobral to Jericoacoara. It is a small pleasant town, surrounded by a *carnauba* palm forest (used in making brooms). At the south end is a large wooden cross dating from 1825, nearby is a statue to São Francisco. There is a lively market on Sunday when, at dawn, *pau d'arara* trucks, mule carts and bicycles converge on the town. There are two very basic hotels.

Western Ceará → *For listings, see pages 108-121.*

Sobral → *Phone code: 088. Population: 145,000.*
Sobral, 238 km west of Fortaleza (four hours by bus, US$5), is the principal town in western Ceará and the access point to beaches in the west of the state. The city has a handful of well-preserved colonial buildings including the **Catedral da Sé**, **Teatro São João** and a mansion on the Praça da Sé. There is a **Museu Diocesano** ① *Praça São João*, a Cristo Redentor statue and a monument to the 1919 solar eclipse. Near town is the **Parque Ecológico Lagoa da Fazenda**.

Chapada de Ibiapaba
Brazil's smallest national park lies in the heart of the Chapada de Ibiapaba mountains in the far northwest of the state. The Chapada is an area of tablelands, caves, rock formations, rivers and waterfalls, most of which is unprotected. There are many small towns and places to visit: **Tianguá** is surrounded by waterfalls; 3 km to the north is the Cachoeira de São Gonçalo, a good place for bathing; 5 km from town are natural pools at the meeting place of seven waterfalls; and about 16 km from town, on the edge of the BR-222, is Cana Verde, a 30-m-high waterfall surrounded by monoliths and thick vegetation.

Some 30 km north of Tianguá is **Viçosa do Ceará**, a pretty colonial town also within the *chapada*, known for its ceramics, hang-gliding, food and drink. Climb to the Igreja de Nossa Senhora das Vitórias, a stone church on top of the 820-m-high **Morro do Céu** (reachable by walking up 360 steps), for a good view of the town, the surrounding highlands and the *sertão* beyond. Near the town are interesting rock formations, such as the 100-m-wide **Pedra de Itagurussu** with a natural spring. There is good walking in the area. Basic walking maps are available at the **Secretaria de Turismo**, near the old theatre to the right of the *praça* on which the church stands. Ask about visiting the community that makes sun-baked earthenware pots. There are five buses a day from Fortaleza via Sobral.

Parque Nacional Ubajara

Some 18 km south of Tianguá, at an altitude of 840 m, is the town of **Ubajara**, with an interesting Sunday morning market selling produce of the *sertão*. Some 3 km from the town is the **Parque Nacional Ubajara**, with 563 ha of native highland and *caatinga* brush. It is the smallest of Brazil's national parks and its main attraction is the **Ubajara cave** on the side of an escarpment. Fifteen chambers extending for a total of 1120 m have been mapped, of which 360 m are open to visitors. Access is along a 6-km footpath and steps (two to three hours, take water) or by a **cable car** ① *T088-3634 1219, 0900-1430, last up at 1500, US$1.50*, which descends the cliff to the cave entrance. Lighting has been installed in nine caverns of the complex. The cave is completely dry and home to 14 types of bat. Several rock formations look like animals, including a horse's head, caiman and a snake; a fact which guides spend much of the tour explaining. In 1979 a speleological expedition found a giant skull in one of the caves, belonging to what was later identified as a previously unknown species of bear related to the Andean spectacled bear, and suggesting that the Serra was far colder 10,000 years ago than it is today.

Ins and outs   A guide from the **Instituto Chico Mendes de Conservação da Biodiversidade** (ICMBio) leads visitors through the cave. At the park entrance is an **ICMBio office** ① *5 km from the caves, T085-3634 1388, www.icmbio.gov.br*, and a bar by the entrance serving juices, snacks and drinks. In the park there is a new easy walkway through the woods with stunning views at the end. Start either to the left of the park entrance or opposite the snack bar near the cable-car platform. There is a good 8-km trail to the park from Araticum (7 km by bus from Ubajara). This route is used by locals and passes through *caatinga* forest. There are six buses daily from Fortaleza to Ubajara town. From Jericoacoara it is necessary to change buses in Sobral (which is itself reachable from Jijoca). For more information, including accommodation, see http://portalubajara.com.br and www.ubajara.ce.gov.br.

South from Ubajara

The Chapada de Ibiapaba continues south from Ubajara for some 70 km. Other towns in the highlands are: **Ibiapina**, with the nearby Cachoeira da Ladeira, reached by a steep trail, a good place for bathing; **São Benedito**, known for its straw and ceramic crafts and a working *engenho* sugar mill; and **Carnaubal**, with waterfalls and a bathing resort.

   Ipu, 80 km south of Ubajara, is a town at the foot of the Serra de Ibiapaba, on the edge of the *sertão*. It's an interesting transition as you descend from the green serra, with its sugar cane, tall *babaçu* palms and cattle, down the escarpment to the *sertão*. Ipu's main claim to fame is the **Bica do Ipu**, a 180-m waterfall plunging off the sheer edge of the *serra* into a pool; it is said to be the site of the legendary love affair between *Iracema*, a local indigenous Brazilian woman, and the founder of Fortaleza. You can cool off under the falls and there are basic facilities and a few places to stay around town.

   If driving, you can cross the *sertão* on good roads via **Varjota** on the large lake of the **Açude de Araras** (33 km), **Santa Quitéria** (a further 41 km) to **Canindé** (111 km on the CE-257).

   Monsenhor Tabosa, in the centre of the state, has the highest peak in Ceará, the Pico da Serra Branca, which rises to 1156m, and which is the source of two of the states principal rivers, the Acaraú and the Quixeramobim. The area around the mountain, in the **Serra das Matas**, has been made into an environmental protection area, with *caatinga* and patches of *Mata Atlântica*. There is good day hiking in the hills – none is available through organized tours so you'll have to take a taxi or local bus from Monsenhor Tabosa (ask in the *pousadas*). This remote town is very friendly, with a a handful of very simple hotels (see Sleeping, page 112). It can get very wet in the rainy season (around March). The easiest way to get there is by car or **Horizonte** bus on the CE032 from Canindé, but there are roads from Nova Russas, south of Ipu, and the BR-020 from Boa Viagem (which is very rough).

Continuing south, the greenery of the Chapada de Ibiapaba eventually gives way to the dry **Sertão dos Inhamuns**. One of the main towns in this area is **Crateús**, about 210 km south of Sobral, a remote settlement with rich folkloric traditions seen during the festivals of **Mergulho Folclórico** in August, and the **Festival de Repentistas**, in September. Nearby are archaeological sites with rock inscriptions. There is a regular bus service on the paved road to Fortaleza (347 km). The bus service from Crateús runs along the very bad road to Teresina, every other day.

South of Fortaleza → *For listings, see pages 108-121.*

The Maciço de Baturité mountains → *Population: 32,000. Altitude: 171 m.*

The town of **Baturité**, the largest in the area, is surrounded by the hills and waterfalls of the **Maciço de Baturité**, an irregular massif with beautiful scenery, many waterfalls and good **birdwatching** (which can be organized through the excellent Ciro Albano, see page 118). Baturité is more in the foothills than in the *serra* proper. It has some colonial buildings and a historical museum and is home to the **Pingo de Ouro** distillery, which can be visited. There are several hotels and restaurants, or you can also stay in the **Jesuit Seminary** ① *T085-3347 0362 in advance*, where a few monks still work in the local community and tend the cloister garden (**$** per person, full board US$11.10 per day including morning and afternoon coffee with local fruits, ask for 'Jesuitas' if taking a taxi, or walk up). The *rodoviária* is beyond town on the way out to Guaramiranga.

Some 16 km northwest of Baturité, is **Guaramiranga**, the centre of a fruit and flower growing area. At 365 m above sea level, it is reached by a very twisty road through lush vegetation and fruit trees full of birds. There are several *pousadas* along the way. The town is packed with visitors at weekends; if you want to stay overnight you must book in advance. During **Carnaval** (February) there is a **Festival de Jazz and Blues**. To ensure a bed during this time you must book in November. The town also holds a **Festival Nordestino de Teatro** in September in the **Teatro Municipal Rachel de Queiroz**. This is in the centre of town and around it are a number of restaurants including **Café com Flores**, **Taberna Portuguesa**, **O Alemão**, **Confrari** (for pasta and fondue). For information contact secultguaramiranga@hotmail.com.

About 7 km further north is **Pacoti**, with large botanical gardens (*horto forestal*). There are trails for viewing the highland flora, and several waterfalls that are good for a dip. On the main road to Pacoti, turn left at Forquilha to climb **Pico Alto** (1115 m above sea level), previously thought to be the highest peak in Ceará, which offers special views and sunsets. You can go up by car, or if you leave early in the morning you may be able to catch a lift with the school bus.

Juazeiro do Norte → *For listings, see pages 108-121. Phone code: 088. Population: 200,000.*

The south of the state is known as the **Cariri region**, the name of an indigenous group that lived in the interior and resisted Portuguese colonization for a long time. The main centre in this area is Juazeiro do Norte, the second largest city in Ceará. Along with its two satellites, **Crato** and **Barbalha**, 10 km to the west and south respectively, they form an oasis of green in the dry *sertão*.

Juazeiro was home to one of Brazil's most venerated Catholic figures: the miracle working priest, Padre Cícero Romão Batista, a controversial and very popular figure who championed the rights of Ceara's poor from the 1870s to the 1930s. Even before his death, Padre Cícero had become a legend after a consecrated communion wafer he passed to a woman at Mass reportedly bled in her mouth, and Juazeiro do Norte an important pilgrimage site, drawing the faithful from throughout the northeast and, increasingly, from the whole nation. Today it is the most important pilgrimage centre of the region and visiting during a pilgrimage is an incredible experience. The town is dominated by the imposing Italiantate **Sanctuário do Sagrado Coração de Jesus** basilica and a huge sombre **statue of Padre Cícero**, gazing at a distant horizon from the top of the **Colina do Horto** hill, 8 km from the town centre. To get there, either take the pilgrim trail up the hill (one hour, start early because of the heat) or take the **Horto** city bus to the summit. There are also two museums devoted to the priest. The **Memorial Padre Cícero** ⓘ *R São José 242, T088-3512 2240, Mon-Sat 0800-1100 and 1300-1600, Sun 0900-1100 and 1400-1700, free*, is based in the house where he lived and preserves some of his personal belongings and myriad messages from pilgrims including lottery tickets and football coupons that provided winnings after Cicero answered pilgrims prayers. There are even more covering the walls of the **Museu Vivo do Padre Cicero** ⓘ *Colina do Horto, daily 0800-1200 and 1400-1700, free*, together with numerous effigies and devotional books. The priest is buried in the simple church of **chapel of Nossa Senhora do Perpétuo Socorro** ⓘ *Praça do Cinqüentenário, daily 0800-1800, free*, which is completely packed with pilgrims during religious celebrations. Also worth seeing is the **church of Nossa Senhora das Dores** with the adjacent pilgrimage grounds, roughly fashioned after St Peter's Square in Rome.

The town receives six main annual pilgrimages (see Festivals and events, page 116), but visitors arrive all year round and religious tourism is the principal source of income. Another cultural manifestation seen throughout the Cariri region is the *bandas cabaçais ou de pífaros*, musical groups that participate in all celebrations. As well as playing instruments, they dance, imitating animals, and perform games or fights.

Ins and outs

Cariri airport ⓘ *Av Virgílio Távora 4000, T088-3572 0700*, is 6 km from the city and receives flights from Brasília, Fortaleza, Recife, Rio de Janeiro and São Paulo (Guarulhos). A taxi to the centre costs US$5.75 (motorcycle taxi US$3); a taxi to the bus station costs US$8.40. The **rodoviária** ⓘ *Av Delmiro Gouveia s/n, T088-3571 2309*, is on the road to Crato. A taxi to the centre costs US$3 (motorcycle taxi US$0.60). ▸▸ *See Transport, page 120.*

Ceará listings

For Sleeping and Eating price codes and other relevant information, see pages 8-11.

🛏 Sleeping

Fortaleza *p93, map p94*

Almost all hotels offer reduced prices in the low season. There are many *pousadas* in the Iracema/Meireles area, but they change frequently. Most hotels in Fortaleza have a strict policy of not accepting overnight visitors except with prior reservations.

$$ Caxambu, Gen Bezerril 22, opposite the cathedral, T085-3231 0339, caxambu@ accvia.com.br. Discounts in low season. Rooms have a/c, TV and fridge. Room service available, breakfast included. Probably best bet in centre, good value.

$ Backpackers, R Dom Manuel 89, T085-3091 8997, www.backpackersce.com.br. Central, basic, shared bathrooms, no breakfast, linen, toilet paper or towels but free Wi-Fi, a helpful owner and a lively mixed foreign and Brazilian crowd. 10-min walk from the beach.

$ Big, Gen Sampaio 485, Praça da Estação, Centro, T085-3212 2066. All rooms have fan, old lino and clean sheets. Cheaper without TV, even cheaper without bath, simple breakfast, OK, but caution needed at night as it's right in thick of the central scrum.

Beaches

$$$$ Beira Mar, Av Beira Mar 3130, T085-4009 2000, Meireles, www.hotelbeiramar.com.br. Newly reformed beachfront hotel with some seafront rooms, others have a side view. Comfortable and safe, with a pool, 24-hr business centre with internet and parking. Good value, especially in low season.

$$$$ Imperial Othon Palace, Av Beira Mar 2500, Meireles, T085-3466 5500, www.othon.com.br. Large hotel on the beachfront with all the usual facilities, business and tourists catered for, pool, sauna, massage (recommended *feijoada* on Sat).

$$$$ Luzeiro Beira Mar, Av Beira Mar 2600, Meireles, T085-4006 8585, www.hotel luzeiros.com.br. A tall tower built at the turn of the millennium and with functional, business-like rooms with perfunctory design touches, a large pool, sauna and Wi-Fi in public areas and rooms.

$$$$ Ponta Mar, Av Beira Mar 2200, Meireles, T085-4006 2200, www.ponta mar.com.br. Aimed more at the business market, but still a good location and similar facilities.

$$$$ Seara Praia, Av Beira Mar 3080, Meireles, T085-4011 2200, www.hotelseara.com.br. 30% cheaper in low season, smart, comfortable luxury hotel with pool, gym, cyber café, French cuisine.

$$$ Casa Blanca, R Joaquim Alves 194, T085-3219 0909, www.casablancahoteis.com.br. The best rooms on the upper floors of this tall tower have wonderful sweeping ocean views. All are a/c, well-appointed (if anonymous) and have international TV. Breakfasts are a feast and there's a tiny rooftop pool, a little gym and massage service. Minivans leave from in front of the hotel to Jericoacoara; if waiting for a minivan, an a/c room costs US$50 for 4 hrs.

$$$ Ibis, Atualpa Barbosa de Lima 660, Iracema, T085-3052 2450, www.ibishotel.com. In anonymous **Accor** boardroom-designed style, with functional furniture, modest workstations and Wi-Fi at a price, together with a small pool. Breakfast is extra and discount rates are available online, pushing the hotel into the **$$** and price range.

$$ Abrolhos Praia, Av Abolição 2030, 1 block from the beach, Meireles, T/F085-3248 1217, www.abrolhospraiahotel.com.br. Pleasant, TV, fridge, hot shower, a/c, rooms look a bit sparse but no different from others in this category, soft beds, discount in low season, internet.

$$ Casa de Praia, R Joaquim Alves 169, T085- 3219 1022, www.hotelcasadepraia.com.br. Well-kept, modest a/c rooms in warm colours and with international TV, Wi-Fi. The best are above the 4th floor and have partial ocean views. There's a little rooftop pool. Minivans leave from in front of the hotel of Jeri.

$$ Ideal Praia, R Antonele Bezerra 281, T085-3248 7504, www.hotelideal.com.br. A mock-colonial hotel in a quiet little back street offering 2 kinds of rooms. Those on the ground floor are decorated with mock-marble tiles and have little windows. Those on the upper floors have ocean views and little terraces. All are well kept, homey and have international TV and a/c. There's a mouse-size pool on the roof.

$$ Ondas Verdes, Av Beira Mar 934, Iracema, T085-3219 0871, www.centernet. psi.br/hotelondasverdes. Scruffy hotel beloved of backpackers even though there are better options nearby. Rooms are musty; be sure to look at several.

$$ Panorâmica, R Idelfonso Albano 464, T085-3219 8347, www.portalde hospedagem.com.br. Very simple peach and grey tile boxes. The best by far are on the upper floors, have partial ocean views and little terraces. In a quiet location.

$$ Pousada do Suiço, R Antônio Augusto 141, Iracema, T085-3219 3873, www.pension-vom-schweizer.com.br. A justifiably popular, well-kept and well-run budget hotel in an excellent location near the beach. It is quiet, discreet and on one of the less noisy streets. There are a variety of rooms, some more spacious than others, a number with kitchens, and all a/c and with a TV and fridge. The Swiss owner runs a decent restaurant a few blocks away and can organize tours and give travel advice. Be sure to reserve mid-Oct-Feb.

$$ Pousada Salinas, Av Zezé Diogo 3300, Praia do Futuro, T085-3234 3626, www.pousadasalinas.com.br. **$** in low season,

popular, a/c, TV, fridge, parking, just across from sea, some English spoken.

$$ Praia de Iracema, Raimundo Girão 430, Iracema, T085-3219 2299, www.hotelpraia deiracema.com. 20% discount in low season, a/c, TV, fridge, safe in room, coffee shop, pool, brightly coloured bedcovers, on corner so traffic outside, but OK for value and comfort.

$$ Villamaris, Av Abolição 2026, Meireles, T085-3248 0112, www.hotelvillamaris.com.br. Plain, simple a/c rooms with cream painted, crinkle concrete walls a tiny work table and international TV. Good location.

Camping

Fortaleza Camping Club (do Professor), R Vereador Pedro Paulo Moreira 505, Águas Frias, T085-3273 2544. Around 10 km east of the airport. Lots of shade, US$7 per person.

Pousada dos Pinheiros, R Paulo Mendes 333, Praia do Futuro, T085-3234 5590, marcosacleite@ig.com.br. On the beach.

Aquiraz and around *p98*

In Águas Belas, there are simpler rooms available in private houses.

$$ Kalamari, Av Beira Mar, Porto das Dunas beach, T085-3361 7500, www.kalamari.com.br. Small beach hotel with balconied rooms overlooking a smart pool. Equidistant between Fortaleza and Aquiraz. Tours organized.

$$ Pousada Mama Rosália Via Local 19, Porto das Dunas beach T085-3361 7491, www.pousadamamarosalia.com.br. Family-run beach hotel with simple tile-floor and whitewash rooms with en suites, a restaurant and a pool.

$$ Pousada Villa Francesa, Av Beira Mar, Prainha, 1.5 km from the beach, T085-3361 5007, www.villafrancesa.com. Tiny 8 room, French-run beach hotel that opened in 2005. Rooms are gathered around a smart pool and the hotel offers tours and internet.

Morro Branco and Praia das Fontes
p98

$$$$ Praia das Fontes, Av A Teixeira 1, Praia das Fontes, T085-3338 1179, www.oasisatlantico.com. Luxurious resort, watersports, horse hire, tennis courts and a simple spa. Recommended.

$$ Das Falésias, Av Assis Moreira 314, Praia das Fontes, T085-3327 3052, www.hotel falesias.com.br. Pleasant German-owned cliff-side *pousada* with a pool and tidy rooms.

$$ Pousada Sereia, on the beach, Morro Branco, T085-3330 1144. Lovely simple *pousada* with an excellent breakfast and friendly staff. Highly recommended.

$$ Recanto Praiano, Morro Branco, T085-3338 7229, www.recantopraianopousada.com.br. Peaceful little *pousada* with a good breakfast. Recommended.

$ Rosalias, Morro Branco, T085-3330 1131. Very simple and somewhat run down but only 50 m from the bus stop, and with a shared kitchen.

Prainha do Canto Verde *p99*

There are also houses for rent (eg **Casa Cangulo** or **Vila Marésia**). Note that prices rise by 30% for the regatta and over Christmas and Semana Santa.

$ Dona Mirtes. Price includes breakfast, will negotiate other meals.

Canoa Quebrada *p99*

Villagers will let you sling your hammock or will put you up cheaply. **Verónica** is recommended, European books exchanged. **Sr Miguel** rents good clean houses for US$10 a day.

$$$ Tranqüilândia, R Camino do Mar, T088-3421 7012, www.tranquilandia.it. A range of thatched roofed, a/c chalets around a smart pool in a lawned tropical garden. Decent restaurant. Italian-owned and with facilities for kitesurfers.

$$ Pousada Alternativa, R Francisco Caraço, T088-3421 7278, www.pousada-alternativa. com.br. Rooms with or without bath. Centrally located and recommended.

$$ Pousada Azul, R Dragão do Mar (Broadway) s/n, T088-9932 9568 (mob), www.portalcanoaquebrada.com.br/. Very simple, small concrete and blue tile a/c or fan-cooled boxes, a sunny upper deck, miniature pool and warm service from the owner Saméa.

$$ Pousada Latitude, R Dragão do Mar (Broadway), T088-3241 7041, www.pousada latitude.com.br. Large a/c 2-storey bungalows in a large complex off the main street. Not intimate but with decent service.

$$ Pousada Lua Estrela, R Nascer do Sol 106, T088-3421 7040, www.portalcanoaquebrada. com.br. A smart hostel/*pousada* with with fan-cooled rooms with great sea views, fridges and hot showers and a/c rooms without views in the garden. 20 m off R Dragão do Mar.

$$ Pousada Oásis do Rei, R Nascer do Sol 112, T088-3421 7081, www.pousadaoasisdorei. com.br. Simple rooms around a pool in a little garden, with polished concrete or tiled floors; some with sea views and some with bed space for 3 or 4.

$$ Pousada Via Láctea, just off R Dragão do Mar (Broadway), www.pousadavialactea.com. This chunky brick building may not be beautiful, but the views are and the beach is only some 50 m away. English spoken and tours organized. Highly recommended.

$ Albergue Ibiza, R Dragão do Mar (Broadway) s/n, T088-8804 7603 (mob), www.portalcanoaquebrada.com.br/canoa_ quebrada_albergue_ibiza.htm. Tiny, boxy but astonishingly cheap and fairly spruce doubles and dorms 200 m from the beach.

Paracuru and Lagoinha *p102*

There are a number of cheaper hotels on both beaches; it's worth shopping around.

$$ Dunas, Paracuru, T085-3344 1965, http://hoteldunas.com.br. Family-orientated hotel with a small water park next door and range of very simple rooms gathered around a pool.

$$ Mar e Vista, Av Francisco Azevedo 170, Lagoinha, T085-3363 5038, www.pousada-maravista.com. The are great views from this clifftop hotel more than make up for the very simple rooms; ask for one at the front with a shared terrace and hammock area.

Jericoacoara *p102*

There are crowds at weekends mid-Dec to mid-Feb, in Jul and during Brazilian holidays. Many places full in low season too. For New Year's Eve, 4- to 5-day packages are available. Prices rise by as much as 40% in peak season (New Year and Carnaval).

$$$$ Vila Kalango, R do Instituto Chico Mendes de Conservação da Biodiversidade (ICMBio) s/n, T088-3669 2289, www.vilakalango.com.br. The smartest option in town with well-appointed rooms in stilt house cabins in a tree-filled garden just set-back from the beach. Lovely pool and bar area, a decent restaurant and excellent facilities for kitesurfers and windsurfers. There's a sister hotel, **Rancho do Peixe**, on Praia da Preá. Shuttle buses to/from Fortaleza.

$$$ Espaço Nova Era, R do Forró s/n, T088-3669 2056, www.novaerapousada.com.br. A mock-Mediterranean lobby house leads to a set of circular a/c or fan-cooled cabins in terracotta brick and polished concrete. These sit in an Italianate garden shaded by trees and coloured with tropical flowers. Room for 5 in the larger cabins making this an economical option. Italian-owned.

$$ Barão, R do Forró 433, T088-3669 2136 www.recantodobarao.com. Duplex rooms in 2 corridors strung with hammocks. All overlook the corridors and *pousada* gardens and the brightest and best-kept rooms are on the upper floors. The *pousada* has a small pool and attractive sitting areas furnished with sun beds. There is a popular *churrascaria* next door. São Paulo owned.

$$ Papagaio, Trav do Forró s/n, T088-3669 2142, pousadapapagaio@hotmail.com, Attractive, stone-floored a/c rooms with pretty pebble-dash bathrooms and hammock-strung verandas overlooking a courtyard garden shaded by prickly pears and with a tiny pool. Brazilian owned.

$$ Pousada Tirol, R São Francisco 202, T088-3669 2006, www.jericoacoarahostel.com.br HI-affiliated hostel with dorms (**$** per person) with hot water showers and scrupulously cleaned doubles (cheaper in low season) with barely room for a double and a single bed. Very friendly and popular with party-loving travellers. Very busy cybercafé, US$3 per hr; 10 mins free use for all guests.

$$ Pousada Zé Patinha, R São Francisco s/n, T088-3669 2081, www.sandjeri.com.br, Simple, a/c or fan-cooled tiled rooms and plain white rooms in 2 parallel corridors. No outside windows, just overlooking the corridor. Cool in the heat of the day, quiet, with decent mattresses and locally owned.

$ Pousada Zé Bento, R São Francisco s/n, T088-3669 2006, Small, tiled rooms with white walls and little en suites off a small, palm shaded and sandy garden annex. Friendly, tours organized, locally owned.

Around Jericoacoara *p103*

$ Rancho do Peixe, Praia do Preá, T088-9966 2111, www.ranchodopeixe.com.br. Chic bungalows set right on the beach next to a long pool. All have hammock verandas and are fan-cooled. Special rates and excellent facilities for kitesurfers and windsurfers.

Tatajuba

There are a handful of very simple *pousadas* in this village between Camocim and Jericoacoara. These include:

$ Pousada Brisa do Mar, T088-9961 5439 with spartan and very basic rooms some with en suites. There are plenty of simple seafood restaurants in town, the most famous of which is the **Barraca de Dona Delmira**.

Cruz p104
$ Hospedaria, R 6 de Abril 314. Very basic, simple little *pousada* with tiny rooms.
$ Hotel Magalhães, R Teixeira Pinto 390. Very basic, shared bath, friendly, meals available.

Western Ceará p104
$ Pousada Doce Lar, R Felipe Sampaio 181, Centro, Itapajé, T085-3346 1432. Clean and comfortable; ask for a room with a mountain view. No restaurant on site but some close by.

Sobral p104
$$$ Beira Rio, R Conselheiro Rodrigues 400 across from the *rodoviária*, T088-3613 1040. A/c (cheaper with fan), fridge.
$$$ Visconde, Av Lúcia Saboia 473, 10 mins from the *rodoviária*, T088-3611 4222. Friendly, a/c (cheaper with fan), good breakfast.
$$ Cisne, Trav do Xerez 215, T/F088-3611 0171. A/c, cheaper with fan, friendly.
$$ Vitória, Praça Gen Tibúrcio 120, T088-3613 1566. Bath, a/c (some rooms without bath and with fan are cheaper), restaurant.
$ Francinet's, R Col Joaquim Ribeiro 294. With fan, bath (cheaper with shared bath).

Chapada de Ibiapaba p104
$$$ Serra Grande, about 2 km from town, BR-222, Km 311, T088-3671 1818. All the usual amenities, good.
$$ Complexo de Lazer Rio's, Viçosa do Ceará, Km 4.5 on the road from Tianguá, T088-3632 1510/1099. Swiss-style chalets, water park, good local food in the restaurant.

Parque Nacional Ubajara p105
$$ Paraíso, in the centre, Ubajara, T085-3634 1913. The best of a poor lot in Ubajara town, with plain, but bright rooms decked out in granite and whitewash, the best of which have small terraces. Rooms at the back are quietest.
$$ Pousada Gruta da Ubajara, T088-3634 1375, portalubajara.com.br/pousadagruta.

htm. Sits just 50 m from the entrance to the park, and has a dozen lemon and orange concrete chalets, some with room for 4 people, and a restaurant serving spit-roast meat, stewed chicken and the owner's potent, home-made *cachaça*.
$$ Pousada Sítio do Alemão, Estrada do Teleférico, near the park, 2 km from town, T/F088-9961 4645, www.sitio-do-alemao.20fr.com. Take Estrada do Teleférico 2 km from town, after the **Pousada da Neblina** turn right, signposted, 1 km to Sítio Santana/Klein (Caixa Postal 33, Ubajara, CEP 62350-000, T088-9961 4645). Herbert Kelin's 5-chalet *pousada* sits in an old coffee and banana plantation surrounded by beautiful cloud-forest, and with sweeping views over the serra and plains. The chalets vary in size. The largest has 2 bedrooms and the smallest and cheapest, shared bathrooms. A generous breakfast is included in the price and **Casa das Delícias** in Ubajara will send lasagne for other meals (the restaurant is owned by Mrs Klein). The *pousada* will pick-up from the *rodoviária* in Ubajara town, given notice. Excursions organized and bicycle hire.

Camping
Sítio do Bosco, 8 km from Tianguá on the BR 222 towards Teresina, T088-9413 0269, www.sitiobosco.com.br. With shady sites, great views over the hills, a cave on site, spring-water swimming pool, restaurant and organized hang-gliding and excursions.

South from Ubajara p105
$$ Pousada de Inhuçu, R Gonçalo de Freitas 454, São Benedito, T088-3626 3232, www.clubepousada.com.br, in Inhuçu village, 7 km from São Benedito and 30 km from Ubajara NP. A welcoming, small, country hotel with 16 modest, white-wall and raw wood fan-cooled rooms all of which have hammock terraces, some of which are large enough for families (children under 5 stay free). The hotel has a sauna, swimming pool

and can organize trips to nearby waterfalls and Ubajara NP.

$$ Queda d'Agua, R Cel Félix 897, Ipu, T088-3683 1885, www.pousadaquedadagua. com.br. An excellent-value, family-run town hotel with corridors of plain but well-kept rooms, all with a shared terrace, a/c and bathrooms. Friendly owners offer a large breakfast and can give advice on excursions in the serra, which is almost on the doorstep. A map on the website gives full details of how to reach the *pousada*.

Monsenhor Tabosa

The town is tiny. There are 3 basic *pousadas*: **dos Viajantes**, **São Sebastião** and **Pousada Gaia**, just behind the cemetery on the road out to Santa Quitéria (T088-3696 1904); ask for Márcia or Honório Júnior. Honório will draw rough walking maps in the Serra and, if asked, can arrange for the *forró* band to play.

The Maciço de Baturité Mountains
p106

$$ Hofbräuhaus, Estrada de Aratuba, Chapada de Lameirão, Mulungu, T085- 3221 6170, www.hofbrauhaus-brasil.com. Run by Wolfgang Helmut Rühle, who has restaurants in Guaramiranga (**O Alemão**), Pacoti and Fortaleza; he speaks German, English and Portuguese. Rooms are homely and each one is designed in a different style (Spanish, Arabic, Japanese, etc). All are very clean and smart. Rooms with veranda cost a little more. Prices are cheaper Mon-Thu (a bargain). The restaurant is German and Cearense. All vegetables and herbs (for all the restaurants) are grown on the property; it, also has a snail farm for the house speciality. Lots of flowers and grapes, far-reaching views over the *sertão*, mini-disco, small business centre, completely safe. Exceptional.

$$ Parque das Cachoeiras, Estrada CE 356, Km 7 between Baturité and Guaramiranga, T085-8886 5575/3302 1416, www.hotelparque dascachoeiras.com.br. One

of the newest openings in the Maciço de Baturité, with very simple, rooms (with no more than a bed and a wardrobe) in a beautiful setting in cloudforest and next to a rushing mountain stream. The owners organize trail walks and excursions into the park and to the Jesuit seminary (which is in walking distance of the hotel).

$$ Remanso Hotel da Serra, 5 km north of Guaramiranga, T088-3231 7088, www.remansohoteldeserra.com.br. A big mountain resort, with serroed ranks of chalets lined up on the shore of a small artificial lake. The complex is set in pretty remnant cloudforest and trails lead directly from the grounds into the woods. There are swimming pools for both adults and children, 2 restaurants and a playground. Excursions are available through reception. Avoid weekend stays which can be noisy. Rooms cheapest on triple or quadruple share. Breakfast not included in the price.

$$ Senac Hotel Escola de Guaramiranga, Guaramiranga, T/F088-3321 1106, www.ce. senac.br. A large concrete complex with a big swimming pool and a pleasant wooded setting, some 500 m outside town up a road from the main street (past Parque das Trilhas). Rooms are all a/c suites, with fridge and hot water and the hotel has a reasonable restaurant. The grounds have forest walks, orchards and an old convent. As the hotel doubles as a tourism school and hosts lots of events it's an idea to enquire ahead.

Juazeiro do Norte *p107*
Expect prices to be higher during pilgrimages. There are many basic hotels and *hospedarias* for pilgrims on R São José and around Nossa Senhora das Dores basilica.

$$$ Verde Vales Lazer, Av Plácido Alderado Castelo s.n, Lagoa Seca, 3 km from town on the road to Barbalha, T/F088-3566 2544, www.hotel verdesvales.com.br. A resort housed in a large modern mansion house next to a water park on the edge of the city.

The 97 rooms are in the annexe – spread along long corridors. All are modern, spruce and orientated to both families and business travellers. Facilties include a games room, pool, internet access, tennis courts, sauna and restaurant.

$$ Panorama, Santo Agostinho 58, T088-3566 3150, www.panoramhotel.com.br. An 8-storey tower conveniently located in the centre of the city with great views from the upper floors. Rooms are simple but fairly well-appointed and with decent beds. The best are the 5 suites. There's a tiny, unappealing pool, restaurant and internet access.

$$ Plaza, Padre Cícero 148, T088-3511 0493. With bath, a/c, cheaper with fan and cheaper still with shared bath.

$ Hotel Aristocrata, R São Francisco 402, T088-3511 1889. A very simple family-run 2-star option in the city centre, with a/c rooms, the cheapest without fridges and a small restaurant.

$ San Felipe, Av Dr Floro Bartolomeu 285, T088-3511 7904, www.sanfelipehotel.com.br. A range of plain but recently refurbished a/c rooms in a little concrete block in the town centre. Those on the upper floors have with a good view of Padre Cicero's statue.

🍴 Eating

Fortaleza p93, map p94
Iracema and Dragão do Mar
2 good areas for restaurants, with plenty of variety. There are many eateries of various styles at the junction of **Tabajaras** and **Tremembés**, mostly smart.

🍴🍴 Amici's, R Dragão do Mar 80. Pasta, pizza and lively atmosphere in music-filled street, evenings only. Some say it's the best at the cultural centre.

🍴🍴 Colher do Pau, R Tabajaras 412, Iracema. Daily from 1830. *Sertaneja* food, seafood, indoor and outdoor seating, live music. Recommended.

🍴🍴 Estoril, R dos Tabajaras 397, Iracema.

Varied food in this landmark restaurant, which is also a catering school.

🍴🍴 Romagna Mia, R Joaquim Alves 160. Very good fresh seafood, pasta and genuine thin crust Italian pizza made by an Italian ex-pat resident of at least 20 years and served in a little garden shaded by vines tiled with mock-Copacabana dragon's tooth paving.

🍴🍴 Sobre O Mar, R dos Tremembés 2, T085-3219 6999, www.sobreomardiracema.com.br. The perfect vantage point for watching the sky fade from deep red through to lilac over the pier and the green sea at the end of the day. Sit with an icy batida in hand (the *vodka com abacaxi* is excellent) or a petit gateau with chocolate sauce under your spoon. But eat your main course elsewhere.

🍴 Brazão, R João Cordeiro corner of Av R Girão, Iracema. The only place open 24 hrs, but the food is not that special.

🍴 Habanera, R Tabajaras at Ararius, T088-3219 2259. Cuban cigars, great coffee and pastries or, as they are known in Portuguese, *salgados*. Try the *empadas*.

🍴 Santa Clara Café Orgânico, R Dragão do Mar 81, at end of red girder walkway (or upstairs depending which way you go), www.santaclara.com.br. Café, delicious organic coffees, juices, cold drinks, plus sandwiches and desserts.

Beaches
Several good fish restaurants at **Praia de Mucuripe**, where the boats come ashore 1300-1500. **R J Ibiapina**, at the Mucuripe end of Meireles, 1 block behind the beach, has pizzerias, fast food restaurants and sushi bars.

🍴🍴🍴-🍴🍴 La Fiorentina, Osvaldo Cruz 8, corner of Av Beira Mar, Meireles. Some seafood expensive, but there's also fish, meats and pasta. Unpretentious, attentive waiters, good food, frequented by tourists and locals alike.

🍴🍴🍴-🍴 Ideal, Av Abolição e José Vilar, Meireles. Open 0530-2030. Bakery serving lunches, small supermarket and deli, good, handy.

Cumbuco p101

Accommodation can be organized through **Hi Life** (see Activities and tours, page 117).

Jericoacoara p102

There are several restaurants serving vegetarian and fish dishes.

† **Bistrogonoff**, Beco do Guaxelo 60, T088-3669 2220. Fish and meat combinations, stroganoffs and a healthy selection of pastas. Convivial atmosphere, very popular in the evenings. Owners from São Paulo.

† **Na Casa Dela**, R Principal, T088-3669 2024. Northeastern Brazilian and Bahian cooking from owners from São Paulo and Rio Grande do Norte, including delicious sun-dried meat with onions, manioc flour, rice and pureed squash. The dining is intimate with tables mood-lit and sitting in the sand under their own private *palapa*. Waitresses are dressed in colourful regional dresses.

† **Sky**, R Principal on the beach. A popular sunset bar and evening chill-out space with tables under the stars, mood-music and decent though somewhat over-priced cocktail standards.

† **Do Sapão**, R São Francisco s/n, T088-9905 8010. Good-value *prato feito*, set meals including a delicious vegetarian pizzas and pastas. Live music. Named in homage to the giant toads that appear everywhere in Jeri after dark.

† **Kaze Sushi**, R Principal. Decent, fresh sushi and sashimi, miso soups and fruit juices.

† **Restaurante do Suiço**, R Antônio Augusto and José Agustinho, Iracema, T085-3219 3873. Expats and locals flock to this lively little restaurant, a few blocks inland from Iracema beach, to eat the superior wood-fired pizzas, fondues and rosti, and sip caipirainha cocktails and cheap, very cold beer. There's table football and live music some evenings.

🎧 Bars and clubs

Fortaleza p93, map p94

Fortaleza is renowned for its nightlife and prides itself on having the liveliest Mon night in the country. Some of the best areas for entertainment, with many bars and restaurants are: **Av Beira Mar**, **Praia de Iracema**, the hill above **Praia de Mucuripe** and **Av Dom Luís**. *Forró* is the most popular dance and there is a tradition to visit certain establishments on specific nights. The most popular entertainment areas are the large **Dragão do Mar** complex and the bars just east of the Ponte dos Ingleses and around O Pirata.

Mon *Forró* is danced at the **Pirata Bar**, Iracema, US$15, open-air theme bar, from 2300, and other establishments along R dos Tabajaras and its surroundings.

Tue Live golden oldies at **Boate Oásis**, Av Santos Dumont 6061, Aldeota.

Wed Regional music and samba-reggae at **Clube do Vaqueiro**, city bypass, Km 14, by BR-116 south and E-020, at 2230.

Thu Live music, shows at Pirata and in the adjacent bars.

Fri Singers and bands play regional music at **Parque do Vaqueiro**, BR-020, Km 10, past city bypass.

Sat *Forró* at **Parque Valeu Boi**, R Trezópolis, Cajueiro Torto, **Forró Três Amores**, Estrado Tapuio, Eusêbio and **Cantinho do Céu**, CE-04, Km 8.

Sun *Forró* and *música sertaneja* at **Cajueiro Drinks**, BR-116, Km 20, Eusêbio.

The streets around Centro Cultural Dragão do Mar on R Dragão do Mar are lively every night of the week. Brightly painted, historic buildings house restaurants, where musicians play to customers and the pavements are dotted with cocktail carts.

Caros Amigos, R Dragão do Mar 22. Live music at 2030: Tue, Brazilian instrumental; Wed, jazz; Thu, samba; Sun, Beatles covers, US$1 (also shows music on the big screen).

Restaurant e Crêperie Café Crème,
R Dragão do Mar 92. Live music on Tue.

Jericoacoara *p102*

There are frequent parties to which visitors are welcome. About once a week in high season there is a folk dance show that includes *capoeira*. There is nightly *forró* in high season at the **Casa do Forró**, R do Forró, a couple of blocks inland from the beach (low season on Wed and Sat only); starts about 2200. This is the centre of Jeri nightlife, aside from the bars near or along the beach like the European-orientated **Planeta Jeri** on R Principal.

🎭 Entertainment

Fortaleza *p93, map p94*

Cinema For information about cinema programming, T139.

Theatre In the centre are **Teatro José de Alencar**, Praça José de Alencar (see page 96), and **Teatro São José**, R Rufino de Alencar 363, T085-3231 5447, both with shows all year.

🎉 Festivals and events

Fortaleza *p93, map p94*
6 Jan Epiphany.
Feb Ash Wed.
19 Mar São José.
Jul Last Sun in Jul is the **Regata Dragão do Mar**, Praia de Mucuripe, with traditional *jangada* (raft) races. During the last week of Jul, the out-of-season Salvador-style carnival, **Fortal**, takes place along Av Almte Barroso, Av Raimundo Giro and Av Beira Mar. In Caucaia, 12 km to the southeast, a **vaquejada**, traditional rodeo and country fair, takes place during the last weekend of Jul.
15 Aug, the local *umbanda terreiros* (churches) celebrate the **Festival of Iemanjá** on Praia do Futuro, taking over the entire beach from noon till dusk, when offerings are cast into the surf. Well worth attending (members of the public may '*pegar um passo*'

– enter into an inspired religious trance – at the hands of a *pai-de-santo*). Beware of pickpockets and purse-snatchers.
Mid-Oct **Ceará Music**, a 4-day festival of Brazilian music, rock and pop, is held in Marina Park.

Canoa Quebrada *p99*
Jul In the second half of the month is the **Canoarte** festival, which includes a *jangada* regatta and music festival.

Juazeiro do Norte *p107*
6 Jan Reis Magos (Epiphany).
2 Feb Candeias (Candelmas), Nossa Senhora da Luz.
24 Mar **Padre Cícero's birth** and one of the biggest pilgrimages and celebrations of the year.
20 Jul **Padre Cícero's death**. With up to 300,000 pilgrims from all over the northeast.
10-15 Sep Nossa Senhora das Dores, the city's patron saint.
1-2 Nov Finados, the city receives 600,000 visitors for the All Saints' Day pilgrimages.

🛍 Shopping

Fortaleza *p93, map p94*
Bookshops
Livraria Livro Técnico, see Dragão do Mar, page 96. Several branches including on Dom Luís, Praça Ferreira, **Shopping Norte** and at UFC university.
Livraria Nobel bookstore and coffee shop in Del Paseo shopping centre in Aldeota.
Siciliano, bookstore and coffee shop in new part of **Iguatemi** shopping mall, with just a bookstore in the old part.

Handicrafts
Fortaleza has an excellent selection of locally manufactured textiles, which are among the cheapest in Brazil, and a wide selection of regional handicrafts. The local craft specialities are lace and embroidered textile goods; hammocks (US$15-100); fine alto-relievo

woodcarvings of northeast scenes; basket ware; leatherwork; and clay figures (*bonecas de barro*). Bargaining is okay at the **Mercado Central**, Av Alberto Nepomuceno (closed Sun), and the **Emcetur Centro de Turismo** in the old prison. Crafts also available in shops near the market, while shops on R Dr João Moreira 400 block sell clothes. Every night (1800-2300) there are stalls along the beach at Praia Meireiles. Crafts also found in the commercial area along Av Monsenhor Tabosa.

Shopping centres
The biggest is **Iguatemi**, south of Meireles on way to Centro de Convenções; it also has modern cinemas. Others are **Aldeota** and **Del Paseo** in Aldeota, near Praça Portugal.

▲▲ Activities and tours

Fortaleza *p93, map p94*
Kitesurfing, windsurfing and surfing
Ceará is one of the best palces in the world for kitesurfing and windsurfing. The major centres are **Cumbuco** and **Jericoacoara**. The sport is also popular in **Canoa Quebrada**. Rental equipment can be found at all 3 (see the relevant section, below). In Fortaleza, equipment for kitesurfing and windsurfing can be rented at some of the popular beaches, such as **Porto das Dunas**. Surfing is popular on a number of Ceará beaches.
Bio Board, Av Beira Mar 914, T085-3242 1642, www.bioboard.com.br. A windsurfing and kite- surfing school. Looks after equipment for you.
Hi Life, Av Beira Mar 2120, Praia dos Diários, T085-9982 5449, www.kite-surf-brazil.com. The best kitesurf school in the area (see Cumbuco, below, for further details).

Tour operators
Many operators offer city and beach tours. Others offer adventure trips further afield, most common being off-road trips along the beaches from Natal in the east to the Lençois Maranhenses in the west.

Ceará Saveiro, Av Beira Mar 4293, T085-3263 1085. *Saveiro* and yacht trips, daily 1000-1200 and 1600-1800 from Praia de Mucuripe.
Dunnas Expedições, R Silva Paulet 1100, Aldeota, T085-3264 2514, www.dunnas.com.br. Off-road tours with a fleet of white Land Rovers. Experienced, environmentally and culturally aware, very helpful and professional staff.
Martur, Av Beira Mar 4260, T085-3263 1203. Sailing trips, from Mucuripe, same schedule as Ceará Saveiro.
Sunny Tour, Av Prof A Nunes Freire 4097, Dionísio Torres, T085-3258 2337, also has a stand on Av Beira Mar near the craft fair. Beach tours and trips to Jericoacoara.

Canoa Quebrada *p99*
Kite Flat Water, R Dragão do Mar, T085-9604 4953, www.brasilkiteflatwater.com. Kite-surfing rental and excursions at Canoa Quebrada.

Cumbuco *p101*
Hi Life, Av Dos Coqueiros s/n, Cumbuco, Caucaia, T085-3318 7195, www.kite-surf-brazil.com. One of the leading kitesurf schools in Ceará. Can arrange full tours from Europe and organize hotels in Cumbuco and transfers.

Jericoacoara *p102*
Buggy tours cost US$44.45 for a buggy to all the sites; contact the **Associação de Bugueiros (ABJ)**, R Principal, *barraca* near Instituto Chico Mendes de Conservação da Biodiversidade (ICMBio). If seeking a *bugueiro* who speaks English, Spanish, Italian and French, ask for Alvaro, the school teacher, who is Uruguayan.
Vila Kalango and **Peixe Galo**, are orientated to kitesurfers and organize some of the best kitesurf excursions in Jeri.
Clube dos Ventos, R das Dunas, T088-621 0211, www.clubventos.com. Windsurfing and

kitesurfing at Preá and Lagoa Jijoca. Equipment hire, courses and transfers.

Parque Nacional Ubajara p104
Birdwatching
Ciro Albano Birding Brazil, T085-9955 5162, www.nebrazilbirding.com. The best and most experienced birdwatching guide in the north-east of Brazil, offering bespoke and scheduled trips to the Maciço de Baturité and other locations in Ceará, as well as further afield in Bahia, Alagoas, Pernambuco, Sergipe and Minas. Speaks English and will pick-up from airports in Fortaleza or Salvador and organize transport and accommodation in an all-in package.

Hang-gliding
Sítio do Bosco, T088-9413 0269, www.sitio bosco.com.br. Hang-gliding from the Serra de Ibiapaba near Ubajara.

⊖ **Transport**

Fortaleza p93, map p94
Air
To get to the airport, bus No 404 runs from Praça José de Alencar in the centre, US$1.50. **Expresso Guanabara** minibuses run from the rodoviária and Beira Mar (US$2). Taxis to the centre cost US$25, US$30 at night (30 mins, allowing for traffic). There are regular international flights to **Portugal** (Lisbon), **Italy** (Milan, Rome and Verona) and the **Guianas** via Belém.

    Airline contacts Air Italy, www.airitaly. it. **GOL**, Av Santos Dumont 2727, Aldeota, T085-3266 8000, freephone T0800-997000, www.voegol.com.br. **Avianca**, www.Avianca. com.br. **TAF**, www.voetaf.com.br. **TAM**, www.tam.com.br. **TAP Air Portugal**, www.fly tap.com. **Webjet**, www.webjet.com.br, **Azul**, www.voeazul.com.br.

Bus
Local Many city buses run to the rodoviária (US$1.50), including 'Aguanambi' 1 or 2 which go from Av Gen Sampaio, 'Barra de Fátima- Rodoviária' from Praça Coração de Jesus, 'Circular' for Av Beira Mar and the beaches, and 'Siqueira Mucuripe' from Av Abolição. A taxi from Praia de Iracema or Av Abolição costs about US$15.

    For the eastern beaches near Fortaleza (**Prainha, Iguape, Barro Preto, Batoque**) and towns such as **Aquiraz, Eusêbio** or **Pacajus**, you must take São Benedito buses, T085-3272 2544, from the rodoviária. To **Beberibe**, 10 a day US$8. To **Cascavel** US$1.10. To **Morro Branco** at 0745, 1000, 1515, 1750, US$2.25. To **Canoa Quebrada** at 0830, 1100, 1340, 1540 (plus 1730 on Sun) US$4.25. To **Aracati** at 0630, 0830, 1100, 1340, 1540, 1900 last back at 1800, US$4.90. There are regular buses to the western beaches near Fortaleza, including **Cumbuco**, from the rodoviária.

    Long-distance Redenção buses from Fortaleza to **Jericoacoara** from the rodoviária 0900, 1700 and the Av Beira Mar at the Posta Telefônica opposite **Praiano Palace Hotel** 30 mins later. The day bus goes via **Jijoca** and the night bus via **Preá**. The journey takes 6 hrs and costs US$25 one way. Always check times of the Redençao buses from Fortaleza as they change with the season. The night bus requires an overnight stop in Preá; make your own way to Jeri next day. A jardineira (open-sided 4WD truck) meets the **Redenção** bus from Fortaleza at Jijoca (included in the **Redenção** price). Several a/c combis a day leave from outside the **Casa Blanca** hotel for to **Jeri** via **Jijoca** (US$50, 4 hrs).

    Nordeste to **Mossoró**, 10 a day, US$30; to **Natal**, 8 daily, US$25 semi-leito, US$40 executivo, US$50 leito, 7½ hrs; to **João Pessoa**, 2 daily, US$40 semi-leito, US$45 leito, 10 hrs. **Boa Esperança** stops at Fortaleza on its **Belém–Natal** route.

Itapemirim to **Salvador**, US$85, 1900, 23 hrs. Guanabara to **Recife**, 5 daily, US$45 *executivo*, US$60 *leito*, 12 hrs, book early for weekend travel; to **Teresina**, several daily, US$40, *leito* US$50, 10 hrs; to **Parnaíba** US$40; to **Belém**, 2 daily, US$65 *executivo*, 23 hrs; to **São Luís**, 3 daily, US$65, 18 hrs; **Sobral** US$10; **Ubajara** 0800, 1800, return 0800, 1600, 6 hrs, US$12; to **Piripiri** for **Parque Nacional de Sete Cidades**, US$30, 9 hrs, a good stop en route to Belém. Ipu Brasília to **Sobral**, US$14, and to **Camocim**, 1120, 1530; to **Majorlândia**, US$7, **Campina Grande**, US$40, 13 hrs; to **Juazeiro do Norte**, Rio Grande/Rápido Juazeiro, 5 a day from 1230-2145, 8-9 hrs, US$50, *leito* US$90. Redenção to **Quixadá**, many daily, US$7; to **Redentora**, 0600,1200 via Baturité. Redenção to **Almofala** 0700, 1730, US$10; to **Cruz** 0900, 1030, 1630, 1830, US$10. Redenção from *rodoviária* to **Gijoca**, US$12, 1030, 1830 and **Jeri**, 0900, 1830, US$10. Tickets are also sold at the Posta Telefônica Beira Mar, on Beira Mar almost opposite Praiano Palace.

Bus companies Açailândia, T085-3256 8525; **Boa Esperança**, T085-3256 5006; **Eucatur/União Cascavel**, T085-3256 4889, run Pantanal–Palmas, Gontijo–São Paulo, São Gonçalo–Belo Horizonte; **Guanabara**, T085-3256 0214; **Nordeste**, T085-3256 2342; **Rio Grande/ Rápido Juazeiro**, T085-3254 3600; **Transbrasiliana**, T085-3256 1306.

Car hire
Many car hire places on Av Monsenhor Tabosa: **Amazônia**, No 1055, T085-3219 0800; **Reta**, No 1171, T085-3219 5555; **Shop**, No 1181, T085-3219 7788, and many more at the junction with Ildefonso Albano. **Brasil Rent a Car**, Av Abolição 2300, T085-3242 0868, www.brasillocadora.com.br. **Localiza**, Av Abolição 2236, T0800-992020. There are also many buggy rental shops.

The coast east of Fortaleza *p97*
Bus Daily bus service to Fortaleza *rodoviária* to **Prainha**, 11 daily, US$3; to **Iguape**, hourly 0600-1900, US$3. To **Caponga**: direct bus from Fortaleza *rodoviária* (4 a day, US$3) or take a bus from Fortaleza to **Cascavel** (80 mins) then a bus from Cascavel (20 mins); bus information in Caponga T088-3334 1485. For bus information in Fortaleza, São Benedito, T088-3272 2544, at *rodoviária*: to **Beberibe**, 10 a day, US$4; to **Cascavel**, US$3; to **Morro Branco**, 0745, 1000, 1515, 1750, US$4; to **Canoa Quebrada**, 0830, 1100, 1340, 1540 (plus 1730 Sun), US$7; to **Aracati**, more than 10 per day first at 0500, last at 1900, last back at 1800, US$7; onward connections from Arati to **Natal** (at least 10 per day), **Recife** (2 per day), **Salvador** (1 per day). **Natal– Aracati** bus via **Mossoró**, 6 hrs, US$7.50; from Mossoró (90 km) US$2.50, 2 hrs; **Fortaleza– Aracati** (142 km), besides São Benedito, Guanabara or Nordeste many daily, US$7, 2 hrs; Aracati to **Canoa Quebrada** from Gen Pompeu e João Paulo, US$3; taxi US$15.

Pecém and Taíba *p101*
Bus There are 11 daily buses to **Fortaleza** and 4 daily buses to **Siupé**.

Paracuru and Lagoinha *p102*
Bus There are 8 daily buses to **Fortaleza** *rodoviária*, US$3 to **Paracuru**. For information contact T085-272 4483 (in Fortaleza).

Jericoacoara *p102*
Bus Redenção buses to **Fortaleza**, twice daily at 1400 (via **Preá**) and 2230 (via **Jijoca**). The journey takes 6 hrs and costs US$15 one way. Always check times of the **Redençao** buses as they change with the season. A *jardineira* (4WD truck) meets the bus and transfers to **Jijoca** (included in the price). *Combis* also run to **Fortaleza** via Jijoca, US$50, 4 hrs.

If heading to **Belém** (US$28.25, 20 hrs) or other points north and west, take the *jardineira* to **Jijoca**, from where buses run to **Cruz**. In Cruz, you can change for **Sobral**; there is only one bus a day Cruz–Sobral, US$7.25, 3-4 hrs, but **Redenção** runs from Cruz to **Fortaleza** several times daily, US$6.40.

To get to **Parnaíba**, take a Toyota to **Camocim** (US$10) from leaving at around 0900; book through your hotel or ask around for buggy or *jardineira* (US$25 per person).

Motorcycle If on a motorcycle, it is not possible to ride from Jericoacoara to **Jijoca** (unless you have an excellent scrambler). Safe parking for bikes in Jijoca is not a problem.

Cruz *p104*
Bus The bus to **Jijoca** goes through town at about 1400, US$4 or US$7 to **Jericoacoara**, wait for the bus by 1330. To **Jijoca** daily at about 1400, US$1.25; the bus meets *jardineira* for Jericoacoara (US$2.20). Alternatively, take an *horário* pick-up from Cruz to **Jijoca**.

Parque Nacional de Ubajara *p104*
Bus 6 daily to and from **Fortaleza** to Ubajara town, US$20. From **Jericoacoara** take a combi to Jijoca and then to Sobral from where there are buses to both Ubabara and Tinguá. 2 buses daily to and from **Teresinha** (onward to São Luis and Belém), 3 to and from **Parnaíba** and buses every hr from Tinguá to Ubajara. 5 buses a day between Sobral (with connections to Jijoca (for Jericoacoara) and Fortaleza) and Viçosa do Ceará (6 hrs, US$21).

The Maciço de Baturité Mountains *p106*
Bus From **Baturité**, there are 4 Redentora buses a day to **Fortaleza** *rodoviária*, 3 hrs. To **Guaramiranga** Mon-Fri 0830, daily 1030, 1700, also to **Aratuba**. Pinheiro, T085-

3256 3729, also runs to **Guaramiranga** and **Aratuba**.

Juazeiro do Norte *p107*
Air A taxi to the airport from the centre costs US$5.75; US$2 by motorcycle taxi. There are flights to **Brasília**, **Fortaleza**, **Recife**, **Rio de Janeiro** and **São Paulo** (Guarulhos), with Gol, www.voegoel.com.br and Oceanair, www.oceanair.com.br.

Bus To **Fortaleza** with Rio Negro, 2 daily, US$17 *convencional*, US$35 *executivo*, 8 hrs. To **Picos** with Boa Esperança, 2 daily, US$5.75, 5 hrs. To **Teresina** with Boa Esperança, Progresso or Aparecida, 3 daily, US$16, 11 hrs. To **São Luís** with Progresso, US$20, 16 hrs. To **Belém** with Boa Esperança, 1 daily (often full), US$70, 25 hrs. To **Campina Grande** with Transparaiba, 2 daily, US$25, 9 hrs. To **João Pessoa** with Braga, 1 daily, US$50, 10 hrs. To **Recife** with Braga, 1 daily, US$35, 11 hrs. To **Salvador** with Itapermirim, 2 weekly, US$17.50, 14 hrs. To **São Paulo** with Itapemirim, 1 daily, US$90, 40 hrs.

Car hire IBM, Santo Agostinho 58, T088-3511 0542. **Localiza**, at the airport and at Av Padre Cícero Km 3, No 3375, T088-3571 2668. **Unidas**, Av Padre Cícero, Km 2 on road to Crato, T088-3571 1226.

🛈 Directory

Fortaleza *p93, map p94*
Banks **Bradesco**, Av Pontes Vieira 357, and Av Santos Dumont 2110, for international ATM. **Banco do Brasil**, R Barão do Rio Branco 1500, also on Av Abolição (high commission on TCs). **Banco Mercantil do Brasil**, R Mayor Facundo 484, Centro, Praça do Ferreira, cash against MasterCard. Exchange at **Tropical Viagens**, R Barão do Rio Branco 1233, T085-3221 3344, English spoken. **Libratur**, Av Abolição 2194, T085-3248 3355, Mon-Fri 0900-1800, Sat 0800-1200 Recommended.

More *câmbios* on Av Mons Tabosa: eg **TourStar**, No 1587, **Sdoc**, No 1073, T085-3219 7993. **Embassies and consulates France**, R Bóris 90, Centro, T085-3254 2822. **Germany**, R Dr Lourenço 2244, Meireles, T085-3246 2833, gja435@sec.secrel.com.br. **Italy**, R E 80, Parque Wáshington Soares, T085-3273 2606. **Netherlands**, Av Pe Antônio Tomás 386, T085-3461 2331. **UK**, c/o Grupo Edson Queiroz, Praça da Imprensa s/n, Aldeota, T085-3466 8888. **US**, Nogueira Acioli 891, Centro, T085-3252 1539. **Internet** Many internet cafés around the city. **Beira Mar Internet Café**, Av Beira Mar 2120A, Meireles, US$2.60 per hr also international phones. Cyber Net, Av Beira Mar 3120 in small mall, smart, US$2.20 per hr. **Internet Express**, R Barão de Aracati opposite Colonial Praia, opens 0800. **Laundry Laundromat**, Av Abolição 3038, Meireles. **Medical services Instituto Dr José Frota (IJF)**, R Barão do Rio Branco 1866, T085- 3255 5000, recommended public hospital. **Post office** Main branch at R Senador Alencar 38, Centro; Av Monsenhor Tabosa 1109 and 1581, Iracema; at train station; opposite the *rodoviária*. Parcels must be taken to Receita Federal office at Barão de Aracati 909, Aldeota (take 'Dom Luís' bus).
Telephone International calls from **Emcetur** hut on Iracema beach and from **Telemar** offices: R Floriano Peixoto 99, corner of R João Moreira, Centro; also at *rodoviária* and airport.

Coast east of Fortaleza *p97*
Banks Canoa Quebrada has a Banco do Brasil ATM but these do not usually accept international cards. **Aracati** has money changers, banks and international ATMs.

Jericoacoara *p102*
Internet There are plenty of internet cafés in town but no banks.

Juazeiro do Norte *p107*
Banks Banco do Brasil, R São Francisco, near Praça Pradre Cícero, poor rates, Mon-Fri 1100-1600, **Bradesco**, R Conceição 503, Centro T088-3512 2830 and at R Sta Luzia 321, T088-3512 2966. No *câmbios* in town. **Post office** R Conceição 354 and at *rodoviária*. **Telephone** R São Pedro 204, half a block from Praça Padre Cícero and at *rodoviária*.

Footnotes

Basic Portuguese for travellers

Learning Portuguese is a useful part of the preparation for a trip to Brazil and no volume of dictionaries, phrase books or word lists will provide the same enjoyment as being able to communicate directly with the people of the country you are visiting. It is a good idea to make an effort to grasp the basics before you go. As you travel you will pick up more of the language and the more you know, the more you will benefit from your stay.

General pronunciation

Within Brazil itself, there are variations in pronunciation, intonation, phraseology and slang. This makes for great richness and for the possibility of great enjoyment in the language. A couple of points which the newcomer to the language will spot immediately are the use of the tilde (~) over 'a' and 'o'. This makes the vowel nasal, as does a word ending in 'm' or 'ns', or a vowel followed by 'm' + consonant, or by 'n' + consonant. Another important point of spelling is that for words ending in 'i' and 'u' the emphasis is on the last syllable, though (unlike Spanish) no accent is used. This is especially relevant in place names like Buriti, Guarapari, Caxambu, Iguaçu. Note also the use of 'ç', which changes the pronunciation of c from hard [k] to soft [s].

Personal pronouns

In conversation, most people refer to 'you' as *você*, although in the south and in Pará *tu* is more common. To be more polite, use *O Senhor/A Senhora*. For 'us', *gente* (people, folks) is very common when it includes you too.

Portuguese words and phrases

Greetings and courtesies

hello	*oi*	pleased to meet you	*um prazer*
good morning	*bom dia*	no	*não*
good afternoon	*boa tarde*	yes	*sim*
good evening/night	*boa noite*	excuse me	*com licença*
goodbye	*adeus/tchau*	I don't understand	*não entendo*
see you later	*até logo*	please speak slowly	*fale devagar por favor*
please	*por favor/faz favor*	what is your name?	*qual é seu nome?*
thank you	*obrigado* (if a man is speaking) */obrigada* (if a woman is speaking)	my name is …	*o meu nome é …*
		go away!	*vai embora!*
thank you very much	*muito obrigado/muito obrigada*	**Basic questions**	
		where is?	*onde está/onde fica?*
how are you?	*como vai você tudo bem?/tudo bom?*	why?	*por que?*
		how much does it cost?	*quanto custa?*
I am fine	*vou bem/tudo bem*	what for?	*para que?*
		how much is it?	*quanto é?*

how do I get to … ?	*para chegar a … ?*		
when?	*quando?*		
I want to go to …	*quero ir para …*		
when does the bus leave?/arrive?	*a que hor sai/chega o ônibus?*		

Basics

bathroom/toilet	*banheiro*
police (policeman)	*a polícia (o polício)*
hotel	*o (a pensão, a hospedaria)*
restaurant	*o restaurante (o lanchonete)*
post office	*o correio*
exchange rate	*a taxa de câmbio*
cash	*dinheiro*
Meal	*a refeição*
drink	*a bebida*
soft fizzy drink	*o refrigerante*
beer	*a cerveja*
without sugar	*sem açúcar*
without meat	*sem carne*

Getting around

on the left/right	*à esquerda/à direita*
straight on	*direto*
to walk	*caminhar*
bus station	*a rodoviária*
bus	*o ônibus*
bus stop	*a parada*
ticket	*o passagem/o bilhete*
ticket office	*a bilheteria*

Accommodation

room	*quarto*
noisy	*barulhento*
hot/cold water	*água quente/fria*
to make up/clean	*limpar*
sheet(s)	*o lençol (os lençóis)*
blankets	*as mantas*
pillow	*o travesseiro*
clean/dirty towels	*as toalhas limpas/sujas*
toilet paper	*o papel higiêico*

Time

at one o'clock (am/pm)	*a uma hota (da manhã/da tarde)*
at half past two/ two thirty	*as dois e meia*
at a quarter to three	*quinze para as três*
it's one o'clock	*é uma*
it's seven o'clock	*são sete horas*
it's twenty past six/six twenty	*são seis e vinte*
it's five to nine	*são cinco para as nove*
in ten minutes	*em dez minutos*
five hours	*cinco horas*
does it take long?	*sura muito?*

Days

Monday	*segunda feiro*
Tuesday	*terça feira*
Wednesday	*quarta feira*
Thursday	*quinta feira*
Friday	*sexta feira*
Saturday	*sábado*
Sunday	*domingo*

Numbers

one	*um/uma*
two	*dois/duas*
three	*três*
four	*quatro*
five	*cinco*
six	*seis*
seven	*sete*
eight	*oito*
nine	*nove*
ten	*dez*
eleven	*onze*
twelve	*doze*
thirteen	*treze*
fourteen	*catorze*
fifteen	*quinze*
sixteen	*dezesseis*
seventeen	*dezessete*
eighteen	*dezoito*
nineteen	*dezenove*
twenty	*vinte*

Index